anxiety
and panic

your path to recovery

PALMETTO
P U B L I S H I N G
Charleston, SC
www.PalmettoPublishing.com

© 2024 by Barbara Spaulding

All rights reserved.
This book or any portion thereof may not be reproduced or used in any manner whatsoever without the express written permission of the publisher except for the use of brief quotations in a book review.

Paperback ISBN: 979-8-8229-5330-7
eBook ISBN: 979-8-8229-5331-4

BARBARA SPAULDING, LCSW

anxiety
and panic

your path to recovery

Testimonials

Thanks to Barb's live sessions and this amazing book, I now feel equipped with the necessary tools to navigate all of life's challenges. While anxiety may still arise, I no longer freeze and feel powerless in a situation. Barb's expertise on the subject turned my life around and I am grateful to welcome a brighter future.

KB

Barbara Spaulding is a great advocate and coach for helping people with anxiety. If you or someone you know is dealing with anxiety, talk to her or join the group. I got my life back.

D.K.

The anxiety relief 6 week group was scary at first. I'm not a group person, but the support and encouragement was incredible. Barb sets the tone and teaches us what we need to find our calm. It works.

B.T.S.

The calm skills have been more helpful than anything I've tried before. I learned I do have calm in me.

D.D.

I finally feel hope that I can beat this anxiety. It is comforting to have a professional who also suffered and believes in our success.

B.N.

BARB has been a lifesaver.... Recently, my doctor thought I might have early Alzheimer's and I went to for memory testing. After testing, they believed I did not have Alzheimer's, but high anxiety. So I relied on BARB as I knew that she specialized in anxiety. After 5 sessions she was able to help me feel like my old self again. She gave me lifelong ways to deal with the anxiety before it happens and also if it does indeed happen in order to stay calm and not let my anxiety make me angry or prevent my brain from functioning. I highly recommend BARB to anyone who has anxiety.....
C.H.

Barbara Spaulding is a GIFTED anxiety, panic, grief specialist and therapist. An amazing advocate on healing from the root cause of these issues, who has traveled this journey herself personally as well.
Barb listens, with kindness and with her own personal experience Barb helped me break down 30 years of anxiety ...
E.C.D.

Monday I had another first in years. I took a 3 hour drive by myself to visit my brother and anxiety and I had a great time. Once I decided to let my anxiety join me it stayed quiet the entire trip. Thank you
M.L.

Everyday since starting group I am pushing past anxiety and regaining control of my life day by day. It is all about letting go.
P.T.J

Dedication

To my amazing, incredible daughters, C.J. and Jenna, who have brought light and love into my heart in "big bunches." Always listen to your unique voice as you continue life's journey. To my husband and sister who believed in me from the first word and appreciated the need to laugh.

To family and friends. I am beyond grateful for all the incredible moments in our shared life. Heartfelt thank you to every client that walked through my doors and trusted me to participate in your healing.

Contents

Author's Note	1
How to Use This Guide	4
SECTION I: Starting Your Path to Recovery	**6**
Chapter 1: My Journey from Anxiety to Calm	7
Chapter 2: Aha Moment	16
Chapter 3: What is Anxiety Recovery?	20
Chapter 4: Changing Your Relationship with Anxiety	23
Chapter 5: Where Do You Start?	27
SECTION II: Building Your Foundation of Calm	**29**
Chapter 6: Awareness	30
Chapter 7: Building a Foundation of Calm	37
Chapter 8: Breath Work	44
Chapter 9: Avoidance	48
Chapter 10: Three Words	54
Chapter 11: The Cycle of Anxiety	61
Chapter 12: Panic Attack, Oh No!	72
Chapter 13: Tracking Wins and Struggles	80
Chapter 14: Defining Your Recovery	85

Chapter 15: Calm Lens vs. Anxious Lens	91
Chapter 16: Practice Schedules	97
Chapter 17: Focus	106
Chapter 18: Self-Talk	114
Chapter 19: Glitches	123
Chapter 20: Feelings 101	130
Chapter 21: Time to Say Goodbye	137
Chapter 22: Life without Anxiety	144
SECTION III: Frequently Asked Questions	**151**
SECTION IV: Welcome to Your Calm Life	**169**
About the Author	176

Author's Note

I wrote this book to help others suffering from anxiety and panic attacks. This book will help you find your path out of anxiety to a life of calm and peace. It is full of hope and practical answers. There is a way out! Follow this book's exercises and you will acquire and practice easy-to-learn skills. You will apply these skills when anxiety or panic hits, reducing your anxiety of the moment and gaining confidence as you go. You will finally learn to view life from a calm point of view, saying goodbye to your anxiety-oriented life. If you practice and follow the lessons of this book, it will change your life. This is my hope for you.

I started my therapy practice in 1985 and have been counseling and coaching individuals, couples, and families ever since. Throughout my career, it became clear that no matter the venue I worked in, anxiety was the single most troubling issue.

I struggled with my own anxiety until the mid-1990s. After years of anxiety and panic, I saw there was a path out. I took the path out and have been anxiety-free for thirty years.

In my family, relatives suffered with anxiety by living limited and restricted lives. One cousin who loved to take road trips was terrified of bridges, often driving hundreds of miles out of her way. If there was traffic, she pulled off the road and waited. She shared she always walked the stairs rather than taking an elevator just in case she felt panicky and needed to escape the enclosed space. I heard many similar stories from clients and knew there had to be a better alternative than living with anxiety.

I researched to better understand my own personal anxiety and share that knowledge. The more I learned and understood about my anxiety the less anxiety I had. I was invited to facilitate an eight-week women's group about anxiety. It was titled, "Manage Your Anxiety or It Will Manage You." We focused on calming the physical body with movement, breath work, and learning to let go. The women reported a decrease in anxiety, although the underlying anxiety remained. The next eight-week series included going to places that triggered anxiety and attempting to breathe and stay grounded while anxious. It helped some of the women, but not all. Others were so fearful, they skipped what they called "scary field trips."

The next eight-week group incorporated anxiety-reducing skills in the physical, emotional, and cognitive realms; this was successful, with symptom reduction and recovery longevity. The group sessions included exercises for physical, cognitive, and emotional healing. We invited mindful trainers, yoga teachers, and massage therapists. Included were practice outings as well as journal writing. What became clear was anxiety is not just about physical symptoms that get our fearful attention, but about much more.

Recovery starts with practical and calm skills to reverse the onslaught of anxiety symptoms followed by reclaiming your life. This book will walk you through this process.

The beginning of this program started back in 1985. Over the years, it has been my honor and gift to support people moving from anxiety into recovery. So many people have reached out and confirmed that the program works and that they are fully reengaged in their life. Along the way they found their true selves and unlocked the door to pursue what gives their life meaning. It has been my privilege to witness as people find their path to freedom. It is my heartfelt wish for you to take your path from anxiety to calm.

How to Use This Guide

Anxiety and Panic: Your Path to Recovery is designed to be used as self-led coaching sessions. Each chapter offers a story, skill, exercise, summary, and calm affirmation. The stories show how others used the skill in their life. It is written in the order found to be most helpful to participants in the anxiety recovery program over the years. My goal is that you recover from anxiety and panic and fully reclaim your life.

There are seventeen skills outlined in the program. Practice all the skills and choose those that resonate with your needs. As you practice, you'll learn which areas need more attention. Part of anxiety recovery is building the confidence to know what you need.

Not everyone has panic attacks; maybe you struggle only with generalized anxiety. People who have panic attacks may also have generalized anxiety.

Anxiety can exist as free-floating or be filled with what-if thinking. Once you are able to remain calm, it won't matter where, when, or how your anxiety shows up.

As you read the book, you will come across symptoms you don't have. There is no need to worry that you will catch a new symptom; they are not contagious. Your symptoms are distinctively yours based on your life experience. The common shared element is the inability to calm down when anxiety or panic surfaces.

Be patient; every new skill takes time. No one learns to play an instrument overnight.

Find a comfy chair, grab a journal and welcome to the next chapter of your life!

SECTION I
Starting Your Path to Recovery

Chapter 1
My Journey from Anxiety to Calm

My first panic attack happened in 1979. It came as a total surprise, and it was terrifying. Panic attacks were completely foreign to me. Even though it has been more than forty years, the memory of the first attack is crystal clear.

I was in a flower shop picking flowers for my upcoming wedding. Standing in the store, holding a bouquet of pink and white orchids, a sudden flash of heat flooded me followed by a jittery feeling. As others were talking, it felt like I was not present, and it was difficult to take a deep breath. Thoughts assailed me. "Is my throat closing up?" An overwhelming feeling of lightheadedness replaced my usual calm nature. "What is going on?" I became aware of how fast my heart was beating.

My thoughts began to race through all the possibilities of what these uncomfortable sensations could be. The discomfort of not knowing immediately created more fear, which created more symptoms. The sense of danger increased, and in that moment, I was overpowered by the screaming thought that I had to run. "Get outside; hurry; go, run for the door. There must be more air outside." So I ran!

Once outside, I let out a sigh and took slow, deep breaths to bring back a bit of calm.

Then a pounding headache started! The physical sensations made it difficult to focus on the moment. The reoccurring question "What just happened?" became my focus. The only thing that made sense was that it must have been a reaction to the humidity in the store, wedding jitters, or maybe even a reaction to the intense scent of flowers. The overriding, scary feeling of the unknown would not dissipate. What brought me back to the present moment was the store owner yelling at me to bring the flowers that I was clutching back into the store. Oops!

That first panic attack was the beginning of subsequent panic and constant fear. The feeling of being unsafe in my body prevailed, and I wondered when it would return. Trying to push the experience as far back in my consciousness as possible failed. This wasn't something I could share with anyone. How could it be explained? I did not have words for the experience. It made sense to try to forget what happened and avoid all flower stores. At that time, I would have avoided anything that appeared to cause those symptoms.

I struggled with panic and anxiety for the next fifteen years. Life was organized around avoiding or fighting panic and anxiety. Relaxing seemed impossible. Constantly watching over my shoulder and being jumpy became the norm. My new mantra was to stay alert in case there was a need to head to the exit. It was easy to become hypervigilant, waiting and worrying that the flower store incident would return.

What-if thoughts ruled my life and made decisions for me. Fears of anxiety and panic grew louder, and my life grew smaller. It made sense to me that if something caused so much discomfort, I should stop doing it. I began making deals with myself and creating little comfort zones. Those comfort zones were as effective as the old nursery rhyme, "Step on a crack and break your mother's back."

In the midst of panic or fear, fleeing was my only coping skill. The fear of something catastrophic happening was intense. I perfected the art of avoidance and taking flight, believing that was the answer. Avoidance provided a moment of relief, but those behaviors were followed by increased hypervigilance and more fear. The cycle of anxiety was paralyzing, and it seemed to have no end and no way out. Fears crept up about dying, going crazy, or jumping out a window. It is unimaginable to me now that jumping out of a window seemed to be a good option. Rather, it was only an option in the illogical mind of an anxious person.

In all those anxious years, it hadn't occurred to me that no matter how bad the panic was or how long anxiety stuck around, nothing catastrophic ever happened. Every panic attack ended, regardless of what I did or thought.

The worst of my panic came at the grocery store. At the time, there was no online shopping. All attempts at creating safety while shopping failed. Here were some of my clever attempts to outwit panic:

- Shop at a different store
- Go to a smaller store
- Shop at night
- Shop early
- Stay in one aisle
- Never go to the end of an aisle
- Always move fast
- Avoid lines at checkout
- Switch checkouts if busy
- Pretend to forget something to leave the checkout line
- Grab a magazine to read
- Rearrange the cart
- If all else fails, leave the cart and head for the door!

Distractions were a temporary fix, and there were times I left a full cart and hightailed it back to my car. Forty years ago, I was fast! It seemed the more I avoided and ran from anxiety, the faster it ran to catch up with me. Anxiety refused to stay contained to going to the store. I dragged it to social events, art fairs, concerts, and the gym.

None of my rules or avoidant techniques made much difference, because anxiety and panic were my constant companions—companions that seemed intent on going everywhere. Anxiety was never about stores or perceived external triggers, but at the time, I was clueless. Carrying the fear of anxiety and anticipatory worry felt like dragging around heavy luggage. When events arrived, anxiety was already front and center, making it easy to walk into more anxiety.

Chicago's car show was an annual get-together for my friends and me. It was a group event, and it seemed it would be safe to attend. There were lots of distractions and no grocery store lines. At the time, it was still unclear if anxiety would appear that day. In my mind, there was still a lot of confusion about what caused the anxiety, and it was important to attend. "I've been to the car show so many times; it will be fine," I reasoned.

On the drive to the show, I had an uneasy feeling—a little inkling, a tiny flash of adrenaline—and I thought, maybe this wasn't such a good idea. Maybe this event will trigger anxiety. But the adrenaline passed, and I ignored the uneasy feeling. The minute we entered the car show, that little inkling turned into a full-blown panic attack.

As adrenaline flooded me, the palpitations started, and so did the panic. I backed away from my friends and stood near the outer area close to the exits. When my friends noticed my absence, I lied and told them that I was at a different exhibit or got turned around. The truth was, I spent my day near the exits, hiding behind a set of bleachers and waiting to get back home.

That day, I realized that anxiety and panic weren't going to stay confined to the grocery store. That realization was a truly frightening moment. My inability to calm down and stay calm was starting to consume my reality. Actively ignoring or denying anxiety didn't work. Hiding what happened at the car show from others left me feeling embarrassed, which led to more hiding.

As the panic attacks and anxiety continued, I slowly turned into someone unrecognizable to myself. Lying to friends was not a behavior I had practiced in the past. It seemed impossible to talk about what was happening, but I knew this couldn't just be stress. Over time, the preoccupation with when and where anxiety would arise ruled me. It became the norm for me to decline activities or hatch excuses about working late. My worry over accepting an invitation was, "What if I have another panic attack in front of someone or break down?"

Restaurant invites brought a host of new fears to the surface. When I accepted a restaurant invitation, it felt necessary to go the day before to check out the seating. Where was the closest exit? On the day of the engagement, arriving early allowed me to claim the table nearest to the door just in case. It was exhausting, so it just became easier to stay home.

One afternoon, needing to purchase a gift, I drove to a local shopping area with stores up and down the street. Shopping malls, the place of my teenage hangouts, were to be avoided so as not to feel trapped. Open areas seemed safer, because I could see the quickest way to run to my car.

Parking at the first store on the block, I shopped, returned to my car, moved the car thirty feet to the next store, got out, shopped, got back in the car, and did the same thing five more times. Concerned someone might notice my behavior, I drove around the block a few times. Clearly this behavior wasn't rational, but my anxious mind was not rational. None of these creative yet stressful tricks reduced anxiety, and it was a fight to continue shopping. When I finished, feeling exhausted and sad, I wondered whether this was going to be my life.

One of my more vivid panic attack memories proved to be the start of my recovery. It was my first experience using the power of breathing to calm down. One afternoon, my husband and I headed to a mall. Feeling brave, I went into the dressing room to try on clothes. The minute the door closed a wave of butterflies took over. My next thought was, "Oh no, how far away is my husband? I have to get out of here."

When I flopped down on the bench, the panic started. First came the adrenaline, then shallow breathing, heart palpitations, and tingles. The butterflies continued, and they were not comforting, beautiful, floating butterflies. These were monstrous, ferocious butterflies with teeth. Being trapped in the dressing room made the butterflies more ferocious. As my face turned beet red and my legs wobbled, it seemed my life would end in that dressing room.

While sitting there flooded with symptoms, all I could do was cry. Tears started to flow, and it forced me to take some deep breaths. It turned out that crying was a beneficial response, and the breathing started to create a feeling of calm. At the time, my mind was racked with fear and the urge to flee. The connection between deep breathing to combat anxiety was lost on me.

The salesperson heard me crying and checked in. Still shaky, I opened the door and ran past her, not stopping until I found a bench outdoors. I'd forgotten my husband was in the store waiting for me, and it was too embarrassing to go back to tell him what happened. There were no cell phones. Eventually, he went to the dressing room area and was told, "Your wife took off, and she left her coat." He found me sitting outside the mall in twenty-degree weather without my coat, too anxious to go back inside.

A few years in panic, I decided to tell my doctor what was happening. She could not find any medical answer. She decided it must be a mental health issue, so she recommended I go to the hospital for testing and observation. Once I was checked into the room, it was clear this was the hospital's medical psych unit. The doors were locked, and the windows had bars. The feeling of being trapped was real. There were lots of restrictions, including no visitors.

It was obviously the wrong place for me, but it was too scary to speak up. Attending all the groups and individual sessions seemed the best way to get discharged. It did give me the chance to rest, but the nagging question remained: "What is wrong with me?" My growing concern became, "Maybe there really is something wrong with me."

At the end of the week, a discharge therapist came to my room. In the session, she leaned forward and said, "I have no idea why you are here; you are having panic attacks and need to learn to relax, nothing more." She even read the description of a panic attack, and it was identical to my symptoms. She called it an overactive stress reaction, maybe a little neurotic. It sounded official. It was a huge relief—finally, a diagnosis. This was something to grab hold of, and it was good to be out of the hospital.

The moment of relief about having a diagnosis lasted a short time. Relaxing sounded like a solid plan; the problem was, I did not have any idea how to relax. The discharge did not include any follow-up or advice on how to disconnect from anxiety or panic. If I knew how to relax, that would have already happened. Anxiety was linked to me, and without skills to calm down, that was unlikely to change.

So, my struggle with anxiety continued on its merry way, taking me with it. Anxiety had a clear plan, and it was not going anywhere. The doctor's reaction and being in the hospital added to my anxieties, and it was time for new rules:

1. Never share this with anyone again.
2. Create more restrictive comfort zones.
3. Avoid what produces fear.
4. Prepare for the worst.

Chapter 2
Aha Moment

About fifteen years into my journey with anxiety, an aha moment occurred. While shopping, I stopped to read a sign in the store and started to feel familiar anxious symptoms. The urge to run was strong, but the exhausted feeling from running was stronger. Slowly moving toward the door, I stopped. Running wasn't working; it was making anxiety worse.

A new thought surfaced: "Anxiety, come and do the worst. Make me panic; make me scared. Just get it over with. No more running." I waited and waited and waited and nothing happened. There was no catastrophic event, no scary panic, and not even a flash of anxiety!

New thoughts started to flood in:
What is wrong with this picture?
What kind of game has this been?

I've been running and fighting anxiety and panic for years.

Has all of this been in my head?

Was I accidentally creating anxiety because of the fear of anxiety?

The minute my fight stopped and anxiety was invited to come in, it dissipated like a deflated balloon.

As tentative as it felt to continue shopping, anxiety did not return. Nothing happened. Walking slowly and breathing quieted my anxious fear. For years, my exercise program included running out of grocery stores.

In all honesty, that lightbulb "aha!" was not a magic wand that ended all anxiety and panic. Anxiety sporadically continued for some time, but it became less of a singular focus. It became easier to start living again through small steps and often with much trepidation. The severity of my symptoms lessened, and I enjoyed little glimmers of calm.

During my fifteen years of being anxious, I was unintentionally practicing anxiety. It took time to practice calmer ways to balance that out. The path to anxiety recovery is in the practice of calm. It will be worth all the work so you can get your life back.

You can do it!

Over time, the cause and way out of anxiety and panic started to emerge. Calm skills started to replace anxious reactions. Shifting focus from running to slowing down, challenging anxious thoughts, and changing scary inner dialogue worked. Practicing calmer skills created calmer days and left room for anxiety. Anxiety still peered over my shoulder, but it didn't have the chance to take charge. I still had questions about being safe from anxiety, but the difference was my ability to say, "Yes, I am safe."

Being calmer allowed for a deeper understanding of how my behaviors and actions had been maintaining anxiety, not reducing it. Using avoidance and flight responses were culprits, creating a feedback loop that kept playing out. Avoiding, fighting, and running were not solutions; they were part of the problem. Adopting calm behaviors in my life meant questioning what-if responses. I final began to understand that focusing on anxiety brings more anxiety, and focusing on calm means less room for anxiety and panic, creating calm.

At the end of my anxiety period, sitting in a movie theater, I became emotional. My husband asked, "You know this is a comedy; are you ok?" For the first time in about twenty years of anxiety, sitting in the middle seat, there was calm inside me, and that felt emotional. Movies and middle seats were previously avoided, and to realize there was no speck of anxiety in my mind was incredible.

During my anxious days, the worry about anxiety would have prevented me from sitting in the middle seat. If I went, it would be an aisle seat, and I would be watching the door in case there was an anxious need to bolt. The movie would have taken a back seat to managing the anxiety that was with me. When you struggle with anxiety, it takes over; it demands all your attention. As we left the theater, it became clear that the path out of anxiety was real, and my anxiety was finally quiet.

The most important part of my story is that I did recover and have not had a panic or anxiety attack in the last thirty-plus years. "How do you know you won't ever have another attack? How can you say you are cured?" For me, having another panic attack seems as likely as the sky falling. My life has been full of stress, losses, medical issues, and grief, and yet no anxiety or panic attacks.

Recovery has meant I no longer make decisions through the lens of anxiety. What-ifs are no longer prevalent parts of my daily thought patterns. Recovery means I am able to identify a full range of feelings rather than anxiety being the singular and most frequent feeling. Once you find your calm, you will always have it. When you can calm yourself down, it will not matter where you are; anxiety will have no power over you.

When my anxiety started, no one talked about anxiety. There were no Facebook support groups, or social media or public discussions about anxiety or panic. Most people with anxiety were isolated and suffered by themselves. It was lonely and embarrassing being unable to control anxiety.

I share my story so you will know I have walked through anxiety and panic and now live on the calm side. You can too.

Chapter 3
What is Anxiety Recovery?

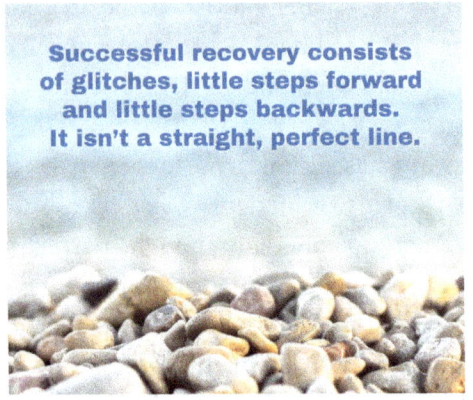

Successful recovery consists of glitches, little steps forward and little steps backwards. It isn't a straight, perfect line.

What does recovery mean as it relates to anxiety? It means living free of anxiety, panic, and obsessive worry. It means making decisions based on what you truly want in your life rather than what your anxiety will allow. It means you knowing the difference between stress and anxiety and striving to live a life of calm, balance, and wellness.

Recovery might look different than you imagine. There may be moments of clarity, moments of emotional chaos, moments of doubt, and moments of joy. Anxiety recovery is about learning new skills that will help you control your anxiety while transforming your life to be calm and healing.

Anxiety recovery doesn't follow a straight line. Recovery is messy and uneven and will go backward and forward. The quicker you embrace the uneven road of recovery, the better your experience will be. Pay attention to your setbacks and glitches, and accept them for the teaching moments they are.

There is no need to judge how long your recovery process takes; your pace and the steps you take will all pave your personal path to freedom and peace. Explore your concerns, feelings, and fears about change and personal growth. Changing is uncomfortable, even when you desperately want it.

Anxiety impacts life emotionally, cognitively, and physically. It creates self-doubt and insecurity. Anxiety interrupts the ability to trust your own body and to feel confident in managing life and ultimately becomes a constant unwanted companion. Recovery includes transforming the areas in your life that have been limited by anxiety.

It is normal to have conflicting feelings about recovery. You may have thoughts such as, "What if it doesn't work? What if I'm disappointed again?" Try reframing these to, "What if it does work? What if I can recover?" You know, if you don't try, disappointment is guaranteed.

Anxiety has been lying to you about many things. It has been telling you what you can't do. Recovery is about what you can do, and recovery is something you will do.

Anxiety has demanded energy and attention, leaving you exhausted. Patience has not been anxiety's friend, but it can be yours, because there is no recovery time frame. It is a healing journey. Begin where you are right now, and move in a new, and calmer direction. At times, the mind is ready to soar and be free, but the body might not be. The shift to a calm and peaceful way of being will be worth it.

Be open to the changes that happen in recovery, be open to not needing to control the pace, and remember to focus on being in the present. It is important to understand the whys of your anxiety without becoming trapped or paralyzed by them. The calmer you become, the more you will learn about what led to your struggle with anxiety.

Take a deep breath, don't forget to let it out, and keep moving forward.

Chapter 4
Changing Your Relationship with Anxiety

"Anxiety and panic cause awful and uncomfortable symptoms. The symptoms ARE real. The good news is the danger is not real."
~Barbara Spaulding, LCSW

Changing your negative relationship with anxiety is one of the most important elements of recovery. It may seem surprising to think about changing your relationship with anxiety, especially since you are undoubtedly thinking, "I do not want a relationship with my anxiety at all." If you suffer from anxiety, you already have a relationship with it regardless.

People call anxiety all sorts of nasty names, from swear words to "evil," "monster," and everything in between. It makes sense, because anxiety takes over the best parts of life and interferes with your ability to function. It is hard to enjoy activities when you are always looking over your shoulder and worrying about when anxious symptoms might show up. Anxiety fills us with shame, inadequacy, and the feeling of being out of control.

In the past, I was angry at my anxiety all the time. I believed if I didn't routinely yell at my anxious thoughts, they would take over. I belittled myself about being anxious and told myself I should just get a grip. Negative feelings crept into my work, the gym, and relationships, and I blamed anxiety for it all.

The more you yell at your anxiety, the more anxious you become. There is no way to recover if the negative and punitive self-talk continues. You must shift your thoughts about anxiety hatred to understanding, and yes, even partnership. Having a positive relationship with yourself is key to having a positive relationship with anxiety. Start with tolerance. Start by not damaging your relationship any further by continued self-loathing. Anxiety does not define you; it doesn't make you weak. It takes a great deal of courage, fortitude, and strength to live with anxiety every day.

My anxiety and I have been fighting for as long as I can remember. I couldn't fight with my abusive parents, so I fought with myself. I could say whatever I wanted to myself and rage at my anger and disgust, and no one could hit me for it. The attempt to exercise control by verbally abusing yourself will not break your bond with anxiety. Blaming and shaming doesn't work. Self-hatred and anger will not make anxiety go away. It will leave you feeling worse.

If we are able to suspend our hatred of anxiety for a moment, we become able to see that anxiety is a scared part of each of us, trying to protect us. Yet anxiety doesn't have the skills to protect, as it is based in fear and is illogical; the result is more anxiety. The way out is to listen and come to know your anxiety, eventually building a positive and loving relationship with it.

When I talk about creating a positive and loving relationship with anxiety, I receive a variety of reactions, including:

"Are you crazy?"

"I came to you to make this monster go away."

"No, thank you; anxiety has caused me so much distress. I don't want to be in a relationship with my anxiety!"

"Can I have my money back? This isn't going to work for me!"

We all have a built-in survival instinct. When you are in real danger, that survival instinct automatically engages, and you know what to do. Fight, flight, freeze, or avoid are ways to protect yourself from danger. You don't spend hours worrying about and anticipating what to do if you are attacked or are in a car accident. If that happens, you react instinctively. And that is a good thing. The problem occurs when anxiety is on constant alert and puts our daily life out of balance. Worrying about situations or symptoms does not protect you and does not change any outcomes. It just makes you more anxious.

If you are at war with your anxiety, you will lose—every time! Being at war with your anxiety means being at war with yourself, and the war will simply lead to more anxiety and more unhappiness.

Take a few minutes and jot down your answers to these questions:

1. What is my relationship with anxiety?
2. How do I react when anxious?
3. What names do I call my anxiety?
4. How do I talk to my anxiety?
5. Do I ignore my anxiety?
6. Do I blame my anxiety for things that happen in my life?

As you review your answers, remember that changing your relationship with anxiety from negative to positive will be an integral part of your recovery.

Chapter 5
Where Do You Start?

You may be asking, "How do I know what I need? I've been anxious for so long, I'm not sure what calm looks like."

Start by increasing your awareness and identifying what you already know.

Many people can recall their first panic attack. Panic attacks are intense and tough to forget. You may be aware of how your anxiety began, or it may not yet be clear. As you start exploring, this is a good time to offer some standard definitions.

I use the word "anxiety" to encompass generalized anxiety, cognitive anxiety, and panic attacks. Generalized anxiety is excessive worry about everyday issues and situations. Cognitive anxiety is fear that stems from thoughts and ideas. Panic attacks are overwhelming, intense feelings of fear that create the belief that you need to immediately escape. Panic attacks also often come with symptoms that include shortness of breath, chest pains, intensive sweating, or even dizziness. It is also common to experience a mix of these anxieties.

"What is the difference between panic attacks and anxiety attacks?" Anxiety attacks are a response to a perceived stressor or threat. Symptoms of anxiety can build and vary in intensity from mild to severe. Panic attacks can be caused by a trigger. These occur suddenly, are disruptive and intense, and cease within minutes.

It helps to know about the differences, but most people use the terms interchangeably. Since many of the symptoms are similar, it is important to know that learning calming skills and practicing calm instead of anxiety will move you toward freedom from anxiety.

As you read this book, there will be symptoms mentioned that are similar to yours and others that are not. It is important to understand you will not catch other symptoms by hearing or reading about them. Symptoms are related to your personal experience and your reactions. My anxiety started with an adrenaline flush, but yours might come with shallow breathing or a sense of being disconnected. Everyone experiences something different. If you feel anxious at any time while reading or working through the exercises, take a break, breathe out, and return when you are calm enough to continue. Listen to what you need as you walk your path to recovery.

SECTION II
Building Your Foundation of Calm

Chapter 6
Awareness

Being mindful isn't about emptying the mind or not having thoughts. Even the word suggests a mind that is full. Mindfulness is about observing, awareness and being in the present moment.

We are not our thoughts, we have thoughts.

Doreen's Story

When I met fifty-three-year-old Doreen, she spoke of her anxiety being a constant, unwelcome partner since middle school. She was not sure how it started; she just knew she could not seem to free herself from anxiety. She said, "Anxiety is always in the shadows, following me around like an annoying younger sibling. I guess I became accustomed to anxiety being part of my life." She didn't avoid places or events, she simply pushed and pushed to do what she needed. Doreen attended social events and never missed work, but she was in a constant state of anxiety. She felt she was losing her ability to keep pushing. The constant anxiety made Doreen feel more and more fatigued. In the group, she shared, "Some days, I think I'm eighty-three and not fifty-three." It was difficult for her to keep up appearances when the anxiety kept her exhausted.

Doreen thought a vacation would help calm her. When she returned, she reported, "I was more tired after a week off from work than before I left. A friend suggested it was probably all my worry and nervousness. It took a lot of energy to hang on to everything."

After all the years of living with the low hum of anxiety, Doreen was missing the most basic understanding of anxiety. She said, "I just put up with it. Maybe I'm too sensitive and it's regular old stress." That is not what anxiety is all about.

When Doreen completed the awareness exercise, she said, "I didn't know how much I was doing that kept this anxiety hanging on. My constant fight to keep it at bay was making it worse, and the more I analyzed my habits around anxiety, the clearer it became that I am at the source of this; that gives me hope. I feel relieved, because now I think there is something I can do about it. I thought I just needed to keep pushing and fighting to get past it. I knew it wasn't working, but I didn't know what else to do. We really are creatures of habit." Doreen was raised to keep her head up and "always keep fighting." The low hum of anxiety had become a squeaky wheel, and she was open to finding a different way.

Skill

Awareness is a way for you to start taking your life back from anxiety. As you work through the exercise, pace yourself. You will find that the more you understand your anxiety, the more it will become less frightening, and you will have a better chance of recovering. One of the contributing factors to how anxiety escalates is the shame and secrecy surrounding it. You can't hide from a part of yourself, and anxiety is a part of you. It has become negative and painful but is still a part of you that needs attention to recover.

This is your story today, and it will start changing tomorrow as you engage in recovery. I dare to suggest you may even come to appreciate your anxiety for the role it plays in protecting you.

Do the following phrases resonate with you?

- "I don't want to learn anything more about my anxiety; it has been ruining my life, and I just want it to go away."
- "I probably can trace the origins of my panic, but I'd rather not. I just want to avoid it."
- "How is this going to help me get my life back?"
- "I'm afraid if I really look at my history of anxiety, I will become more depressed than I already am about being so anxious."

Sound familiar? These are all common and understandable reactions to the thought of facing anxiety head-on. Holding your hands up to avoid it or hiding your head in the sand will only tell your anxiety it is still in charge and create more fear. Anxiety is simply a feeling, not a monster.

Anxiety is a part of you that you want to hide from, avoid, and run away from as fast as possible.

Maybe you have attempted to deal with it in those ways, and here you are.

Exercise

This is your opportunity to write your anxiety story. Feel free to be as creative as you want. It is your story, after all. Here are a few formatting options: a journal, a timeline, bullet points, art, or poetry. Use pencils, crayons, markers—whatever fits you. The questions will help you get started. If it feels overwhelming, just put pen to paper and write "My Anxiety Story" and go on.

- What is your earliest memory of anxiety?
- Has it been constant or intermittent?
- Do you have general anxiety?
- Are you a worrier?
- Describe your anxious symptoms.
- How much of the time are you anxious?
- Is there anyone in your immediate family that suffers from anxiety or panic?
- Is anxiety impacting your social activities?
- Is it affecting your relationships?
- List your five loudest what-if thoughts.
- Do you avoid anything due to anxiety? If yes, what?
- Do you use fight, flight, freeze, or a combination?

Anxiety Scale 1–10

Create a scale to identify your anxiety levels. It becomes a useful guide in assessing progress and being able to identify how much or how little anxiety is present. The scale provides structure to the anxious chaos. When you are at an anxiety level of 3 or 4, you need to start employing your calm skills so you can keep anxiety from spiking. If you wait until anxiety is at 6 or 7, it will take longer to bring it down, and it means you have been practicing anxiety, not calm.

This is subjective, and I encourage you to write a scale for yourself. A few examples:

Anxiety Scale 1–10: Example 1
1. No anxiety, calm
2. Little discomfort
3. Awareness of symptoms
4. Not disturbing
5. Escalating symptoms
6. Looking for a way out
7. More disturbing symptoms
8. Want to run from self
9. Intense discomfort
10. Fears set in

Anxiety Scale 1–10: Example 2
1. Just thinking about anxiety and panic
2. Noticing a little adrenaline
3. Burning adrenaline
4. What-if thoughts starting to escalate
5. My legs feel wobbly
6. Feeling trapped
7. Need to get out of here
8. Heart racing
9. Catastrophic fears
10. That's it! I'm calling 911.

Doreen's Resolution

Doreen utilized what she learned in the awareness exercise to begin to understand anxiety and start building confidence to stop fighting. She said she slept for an entire weekend. She spent three days sleeping, reading, cooking, watching TV, writing, and making jewelry. These were things she had stopped giving to herself. She was resetting her life and taking much-needed self-care time. No phones, no emails—just quiet. She came out of her three-day retreat with a renewed sense of what she needed to do to complete her recovery. After a few sessions, Doreen returned to her life committed to slowing down and using her new skills to avoid the push—the fight mode—she had been living in.

Summary

Awareness is the first step in recovery, and it can be challenging. Recovery requires breaking old patterns and creating new ways of being. Even though anxiety makes us miserable, there is a sense of comfort in the familiar.

If you have tried to share your story with others, you may have been met with a lack of understanding. Maybe you heard comments like, "Everyone has stress," "Just get over it," or, "Just relax." Those comments inevitably make you feel worse and more likely to keep anxiety a secret, silently suffering.

That's why awareness is about you taking back your life. It's about shining a light on your anxiety. It's not your fault, and you haven't done anything wrong to bring it on. You already know running away from anxiety and self-blame doesn't move you to freedom from anxiety, because it can run as fast as you can. Anxiety doesn't feel shamed or blamed; you do. You can break the legacy of shame and embarrassment around anxiety, and you can heal.

Writing your story is a step in owning your experience and giving it value. This is a path to freedom from anxiety, allowing you to keep moving forward.

Calm Affirmation

I allow myself the time I need after writing to sit quietly, take a few deep breaths, be aware of any anxious sensations, and continue to be present and grateful.

Chapter 7
Building a Foundation of Calm

> When you are in recovery each drop of progress counts. Recovery is about lots of small wins that add up to freedom! Celebrate your wins, let go of the struggles. Nourish and care for yourself with love and kindness.

Jodi's Story

Jodi, a fifty-five-year-old, had been anxious on and off for the last thirty-two years. "Some things have helped, but never for more than a few months. I always find my way back to anxiety." After discussing her past attempts, we determined that she had not built a solid "foundation of calm." She had calm skills, but they were disjointed, and she wasn't sure when to use them, which left space for anxiety. Jodi knew four different breathing techniques, but when anxious, she felt confused about which one to pick. Jodi had relied heavily on staying busy when anxious. She played solitaire and read books, magazines, and newspapers to keep busy to avoid her anxiety.

Jodi negotiated, begged, and cajoled her anxiety: "I tell myself, if I get through this lunch, I won't go out to lunch again. I begged anxiety to let me be calm in meetings. I don't know when I started negotiating with anxiety, but it was a technique that worked—for a while."

Jodi started to build a solid bridge from anxiety to calm. She started with one breathing technique, reframed her what-ifs, and relied on her "calm lens" to imagine how she wanted to be. "The Cycle of Anxiety was my biggest surprise. I could match the anxious symptoms to calm symptoms and relied on that often."

As her calm skills became integrated and more natural, she started to connect with her family history. "My mother was the angry parent, and my father was the anxious parent. They tried but did a poor job hiding their struggles. I was closer to my father, so I took the anxious route, and my sister is the angry one. I wish I had picked angry instead!"

Skill: Foundation of Calm

A foundation of calm gives anxiety sufferers a framework for their calm skills. It creates a bridge from anxious reactiveness to a life of calm. Anxiety feels chaotic and out of control. If the foundation of calm is shaky, it will not be there when you need it most—when anxiety or panic strikes. The best way to make the foundation of calm solid is through practicing calm skills and making changes that move you from anxious to calm.

All of you have some skills or strategies that you can enhance or revive for your recovery. You will be building new calm skills as you let go of skills that do not work. At first, being calm will be unfamiliar, like using a muscle that has been sleeping. It needs to be awakened. The more you practice calm skills and behaviors, the more familiar and natural being calm will become.

One approach to anxiety is to shift from reacting to being an observer. When you observe anxiety, you can think through and identify which calm skill will work. It puts you back in charge. Observation allows you to stop chasing or being dragged down the road after every anxious thought. Everyone has a part of them that is already calm; it may not always be accessible, but it is there.

If you are struggling with anxiety today, you are working with a foundation built on anxiety and fears. Building a foundation of calm replaces the anxious foundation with one built with a stable and secure structure.

Think of building a bridge to support the move from anxiety to calm. The bridge provides steps from the constant what-ifs to what-if-nots. It is hard to let go of anxiety without moving toward something else. Having an anxious foundation creates all kinds of havoc in your life, whereas a foundation of calm leads to recovery. This bridge supports you to take the steps needed to build a calm way of living.

A foundation of calm requires solid building blocks. At times, even though you may be in recovery, anxiety will find a way back into your life. It is disappointing, and there are many reasons calm didn't stay in place.

Here are several reasons anxiety may return:
- Not fully integrating your calm skills
- The belief that anxiety left because you got lucky, and now your luck ran out; luck will never stand the test of time
- The belief that if you were lucky, you wouldn't have had anxiety in the first place
- Lacking a particular skill
- Missing a particular understanding about anxiety
- Misunderstanding what is needed to be calm
- Not enough calm practice
- Glitches throw you backward
- The belief or mindset that you can't recover
- The belief that something is inherently wrong with you

These issues can be remedied with skill-learning and calm practice. You are not destined to be anxious forever. That is your fear talking.

The pattern of being anxious reinforces anxiety, and the fear of anxiety is fuel for more anxiety. By focusing on building a foundation of calm, there is less and less room for anxiety. Remember, you have been practicing and reinforcing anxiety. Once you start using your calm skills, your practice will shift to building and maintaining calm.

Exercise: Calm You

1. Think about your calm part. Your first reaction may be, "I don't have any calm in me." Keep looking. It may have simply become buried.

2. What does calm mean to you?
3. When were you calm in the past?
4. What do you know about the calm in you?
5. When are you the calmest—with a pet, helping a young child, doing an activity, with a friend?
6. What do you notice about yourself during those calm times?
7. Describe how calm feels in your body, thoughts, actions, and behaviors.
8. What calm words can you use in place of anxious words?
9. What would being calm all the time look like for you?

Jodi's Resolution

An important part of Jodi's recovery was connecting her past with her present and identifying what was missing for her to remain calm. As she put the pieces together, a clear picture formed that she had built enough skills to make her foundation of calm solid. The need for distractions dropped off as new calm skills took their place.

Jodi took up race walking, which calmed her overwhelm. "Social events and meetings don't bother me anymore as long as I stay grounded."

Jodi came to understand through letter writing that her anxiety was trying to protect her from the anger she saw at home. Her mother's anger scared her when she was a child, and her anxiety tried to protect her. Her anxiety told her not to speak out, not to be noticed, to be perfect, and to stay alert.

Jodi had been dating Tom for a few years and started to see that he was angry most of the time. "Tom is nice; everyone likes him. But under the surface, he is a boiling kettle of repressed anger, and I can't fix him anymore than I could fix my mother. I broke up with him until he worked on his anger. I am done fixing others."

Setting healthy boundaries is part of recovery. Jodi always thought she would be better off being angry instead of anxious; in recovery, she decided balancing all of her emotions was the best option.

Summary

When you are anxious, you develop a foundation of anxiety. You view the world through an anxious lens, you react anxiously, and you fight with anxiety. If you keep giving anxiety negative attention, you reinforce and strengthen anxiety. As you build calm skills, you change your foundation from anxious to calm.

Each of your foundations of calm will be different. They will be a compilation of the calm skills you need for recovery. When a foundation of calm is in place through knowledge and practice, it feels solid. It helps you to be calm anytime, anywhere, no matter what. Anxiety will no longer have a hold on you. If you have a flash of anxiety, that foundation will be enough to put the anxious fire out.

Recovery is an internal process—an inside job. It is not about triggers or external chaos.

A foundation of calm is the backbone of your recovery.

Calm Affirmation

My calm foundation is within me. I believe in my ability to use it when I need it most. In this moment, I am calm. In each moment, I choose calm.

Chapter 8
Breath Work

Remember to breathe out first when you enter a stressful space. Breathe out anxiety, and breathe in calm.

Jack's Story

Jack had struggled with agoraphobia for years. When he joined the anxiety recovery group, he shared, "I feel like not trying anymore, just living my life indoors. At least I can work from home." He explained how paralyzed by fear he was when he stepped outside. Just the thought of crowded places, open spaces, and bright lights sent him into an anxious state. Jack had not been able to previously share his struggle with others who could truly understand him. The group support allowed Jack to start making small changes.

One day, Jack closed his eyes, exhaled, and opened the front door. With every step outside, he focused solely on his breath. He inhaled through his nose then exhaled out of his mouth. His breath kept him grounded in the present moment. He didn't worry about being outside and walking further away from his house. Instead, he kept practicing his breathing technique. The only thing that mattered to him was staying in that moment.

The simple act of focusing on his breath taught Jack he could navigate any situation no matter how he felt.

Skill

Your breathing pattern can serve as a barometer for your anxiety levels. Shallow and rapid breathing indicates an anxious state. These breathing patterns are necessary when you're in real danger. If you have to run for your life, you need to breathe rapidly. If you attempt to control fear by holding your breath, it pushes anxiety levels higher. Your breath is directly connected to your anxiety level.

As you read the stories and exercises in this book, you may notice you are breathing anxiously. If that happens, take the time to practice calm breathing and notice your anxiety.

Here is a calm breathing technique:
- Start by exhaling. This immediately interrupts the anxious pattern.
- It is important to breathe out first to let out any excess air already in your lungs. Breathe in and exhale slowly. Do not take in too much air at first.
- Allow your breathing to return to its natural state. Your body knows how to breathe.

- Continue exhaling and inhaling until you feel you have returned to calm breathing.

To interrupt anxious breathing, bring your body back to its normal way of breathing. This is the quickest and most direct route to get to calm. It is important to use the same method repeatedly. "Sometimes, just remembering to breathe is all I can do." Being calm is about letting the body do what it is naturally designed to do. This brings your body back to homeostasis with respect to your breathing, heart rate, blood flow, and centeredness. Placing your hand over your heart helps you stay connected and invites calm.

By harnessing the power of your own breath, you are taking the first step toward recovery.

Exercise

What are your anxious breathing patterns?

- Is your breath shallow?
- Do you hyperventilate?
- Do you struggle to take a deep breath?
- Do you yawn excessively?
- Is there tightness in your chest?
- Do you hold your breath?
- Do you speak quickly?

Once you identify which anxious breathing techniques you employ, practice incorporating calm breathing into your daily routine.

Jack's Resolution

Jack continued to practice his breathing technique, using it to ground himself in the present moment. He focused on exhaling a heavy sigh to physically release his anxiety.

One day, Jack's anxiety rose. He started breathing shallowly while walking his dog, and he wanted to run! He remembered his breathing technique and started doing it. It was hard at first as his anxiety was high. As he did it, he noticed he calmed down. He realized he was in control of his anxiety and that he could calm himself down!

Jack continued practicing his breathing technique, which resulted in fewer anxious episodes. He reported this to the rest of his group. They congratulated Jack for turning the corner on his anxiety.

Today, Jack inhales calm through his nose and exhales anxiety through his mouth. He practices this technique when he is calm, so he is able to move into it automatically when he is anxious.

Summary

Anxiety is a learned experience often picked up in childhood. It is important to remember that your environment is where you observe and adopt your habits, whether they are good or bad. You can change previously learned anxious reactions to cultivate a sense of calm by using your breath. As your body transitions to a calmer state, it may feel unfamiliar, but once you practice regularly, it will become second nature.

Your new normal will be what you practice. This process is transformative. Breathing grounds you in the present moment, helps you embrace the new sense of calm, and creates inner peace and quiet.

Calm Affirmation

I use my breath to calm myself. I breathe out anxiety, and I breathe in calm. My breath helps maintain calm. Calm breathing is at the center of my calm practice.

Chapter 9
Avoidance

Gwen's Story

Gwen gave a perfect example of how avoidance caused her anxiety to be on high alert. "I was at work and received our company picnic invite, scheduled in two weeks. I thought about what to bring and was excited about attending. Immediately after sending in my RSVP, I had an uneasy feeling. My next thought was, since the picnic was outdoors, if I got anxious, I could leave. I wanted to be able to attend the picnic like everyone else. Ignoring anxiety didn't work.

"The week before the picnic, worry and catastrophic fears continued. That what-if thought became louder and more persistent. The uh-ohs followed, and I started imagining ways to get out of going. The doubts became more obsessive, and I wondered if I should go at all. Eventually the thought, 'What if I have a panic attack?' surfaced. What if I feel wobbly and need to sit down or leave and can't find the exit? It would be embarrassing to get anxious at a work event. 'What if...what if...' persisted until I couldn't imagine going to the picnic at all."

Gwen realized her anxious thoughts had begun a week before the picnic, and she knew she needed to intervene immediately to stop the what-ifs from snowballing. Her first anxious thought was, "The picnic is outdoors, so I can leave if I need to." By creating a back door in case she got anxious, she essentially told her anxiety to be on guard and ready to flee.

Gwen continued to avoid her anxious thoughts, fueling more anxiety. Her anxiety overwhelmed her, and avoidance was her coping mechanism of choice. She had struggled with anxiety and panic for twenty years. Gwen said, "Avoidance and I are old friends or enemies, depending on the day. Sometimes I force myself to attend an event, but then I'm too anxious to enjoy it."

By the time the day of the picnic arrived, Gwen was so exhausted by worry, she stayed home. Staying home made her feel defeated and filled with shame. She wanted to go to the picnic, but her anxiety didn't. "My anxiety generally wins. I end up being the loser, but it's easier than fighting."

Gwen began to respond to her anxiety the moment it started rather than ignoring it. At first, it was difficult for her to listen without getting scared. Listening and offering comfort through calm breathing gave her a sense of control. In a writing exercise, Gwen realized she had used avoidance as a child. "I remember in grammar school when I had tests or field trips, I would get anxious and have an upset stomach. My parents tried to help by letting me stay home, starting a pattern of avoidance. I don't think they knew what else to do. My mom and I would spend the day at home talking and cooking, and I felt safe. Nobody saw the long-term impact."

Gwen had been avoiding her anxiety for so many years, she wasn't sure what it was like not to be anxious. Instead of ignoring or avoiding her anxious reaction, she learned to take a step back and observe. She practiced sitting with her anxious sensations when they arose and over time became less inclined to avoid. "I am truly surprised that anxiety isn't as bad as I imagined it. It feels like a gentle wave, not a tsunami."

Skill

Handling avoidance can be tricky because there is a moment of relief when you avoid. "Phew, I dodged getting anxious at that party by not attending." After the quick relief, most people experience remorse and sadness. Next time it will be harder because avoidance sets you up for a continuing struggle.

Most people try fighting or fleeing from their anxiety. Avoidance isn't only about events. Avoidance can be applied to conversations, medical appointments, not making your needs known, and procrastination. Avoidance sets us up to believe that we can't do things because we might get anxious or panicked. Avoidance keeps the anxious fire on simmer, quiet but always in the background. It feeds the anxious mind with fears and keeps you stuck.

As you learn to be with your anxiety rather than avoid it, you will find it is not so overwhelming. This may seem impossible at first, but little by little, you will learn to be with your anxiety. This is your road to recovery.

Statements about avoiding anxiety are filled with lies. Challenging lies and catastrophic fears will help you discern what is true and what is not. The lie is "I can't do it," rather than the truth: "I'm scared."

You are learning to replace lies with calm skills as you progress through this book. Remember that broken coping mechanisms do not lessen anxiety. Chapter by chapter, you are building your skills to handle your anxiety.

Recovery is knowing when you do not attend an event, it is because you don't want to, not because you are too scared or anxious to attend.

Exercise

Questions to answer:
- What things do you avoid because of anxiety?
- How long have you been avoiding them?
- What are your backdoor escape routes?
- Where are your comfort zones?
- How often do you avoid?
- How does it feel when you avoid?
- What do you tell yourself about avoiding?

Listen to your answers with curiosity, understanding, and compassion.

The following is an example of how to apply the exercise to your specific avoidance areas.

Example: Avoid Going to the Gym

What is your dialogue around avoiding the gym?

- Describe what you believe will happen if you go to the gym.
- Has it happened before?
- What is the worst that you think will happen?
- How likely is it to happen?
- Can you survive the worst?
- How would you like to be when you go to the gym?

Gwen's Resolution

Gwen was successful in turning around her avoidant behaviors by understanding the true nature of her anxious thoughts. She reported, "The New Year's Eve party was in a hotel on the fifteenth floor, and I acknowledged all my huge what-ifs instead of ignoring them. I even invited the anxiety to present itself so I could use my calm skills. Anxious thoughts were there at first, but I didn't let them choose what I would do, and I didn't avoid the party. That worked! I attended the party and had a great time. This year, I volunteered to help plan the company picnic."

Summary

Setting up false comfort zones or backdoor escape routes are forms of avoidance. Anxiety will not be contained that way. As you practice and gain more calm skills, you won't need to avoid. Anxiety is always in sleep mode in our mind; avoidance is one way you wake it up. If you counter anxious thoughts with calm thoughts, you can keep anxiety in sleep mode.

Avoidance sends a scared signal, which creates more anxiety. It generates a sense of being unsafe. As you are able to calmly attend previously avoided events, it becomes easier to let go of back doors and comfort zones.

There may be a time when you are not up to doing something and will avoid it. If you find you must avoid something, try to tell yourself, "I cannot do this yet, and I choose to avoid it." At least you will be making the choice without letting anxiety make the decision.

When you learn not to trust your own experiences, it can be the start of anxious patterns. As you reconnect during recovery, you will find your voice and regain the ability to trust. You are your own expert, even if your ability to listen has been blocked.

Calm Affirmation

Avoiding is an old behavior that I no longer need. I have calm skills and the ability to comfort myself, and I listen to me.

Chapter 10
Three Words

> **3 WORDS**
>
> Three words are easy to remember when you get anxious.
> Use words that will counteract your physical, emotional and cognitive.
>
> Breathe, focus, I'm safe
> Breathe, slow down, focus
> Breathe, let go, I'm ok
> Focus, float, let go

Danny's Story

Danny, a fifty-six-year-old attorney, reached out for help because he was struggling with increased anxiety. He could not identify specific details or describe his anxiety. "I feel a big sense of doom; it's a thundercloud following me. My worry is over the top. It moves from one thing to another at lightning speed, making it hard for me to focus. I think if I slow down, it will swallow me." He was having trouble sleeping, which further affected his concentration.

Danny ran a successful law firm with twenty employees and believed his job required him to move at hyperspeed. If he tried to slow down, worries overwhelmed him, and he imagined a darkness closing in.

In the evenings, he felt pressure in his chest, had trouble catching his breath, and was exhausted. His doctor had cleared him medically and told him he needed to calm down. Danny laughed—kidding—that he needed a different doctor. "I don't have time to calm down, and even if I did have time, I don't know how."

Danny had trouble sitting still in sessions and needed a way to quiet his anxious energy so he could begin the work of recovery. He admitted quiet made him uncomfortable. With practice, he was able to use breathing exercises to decrease his anxious energy and increase his focus.

Danny's next calm skill was creating three words that he could focus on when he felt doom and worry. He picked *breathe*, *focus*, and *slow*. "I thought the three words were too easy; how could they possibly calm me down when I'm an anxious bundle? At first, I didn't remember all three words, even forgot where I stored them in my phone. Practicing when I wasn't anxious made the difference. The first time I used them when anxious, they worked."

When his worry surfaced, he repeated his words, often needing ten repetitions or more before he could calm down. As Danny repeated his three words and practiced calm breathing, he noticed his concentration improving.

Danny described himself as the designated family worrier, second in line to his dad. "We had an unconventional family. My mom worked outside the home, and Dad worked at home. My dad learned to cook growing up in Italy, and he taught me how to cook and how to worry. Unfortunately, I was a good student in both."

There was an eight-year age difference between Danny and his three younger siblings, and he helped raise them. His mother traveled an hour to and from work, so Danny had childcare responsibilities after school, including homework and meal help. He enjoyed it for the most part but took on some of the worry along with the responsibilities. His mother was present physically but overwhelmed with work struggles.

Danny recalled an incident when he was twelve. There was a huge snowstorm, and his mother had been on the road for hours since leaving work. This was before cell phones, and his father was pacing in the front window, worrying that she had been in a crash. When Danny asked what was wrong, his father snapped at him and said, "Nothing, just leave me alone." All Danny knew was something must be wrong, but he didn't understand it. As a kid, a snowstorm was a fun day off school with playing in the snow and hot chocolate. It meant something entirely different to an adult driving home in a snowstorm. "Seeing my father's fear that day scared me, but I had no way to talk about it. You didn't talk about feelings. I remember it as my first lesson in fear. I decided that when I got scared, I should keep it to myself and just deal with it."

Skill

When you get anxious, it is hard to remember anything. You feel confused, frozen, or overwhelmed. If you are stuck in anxiety, your reaction will be to fight, freeze, or take flight. It won't be a rational, calming thought. Anxiety floods the mind with what-ifs, making it hard to focus or solve problems.

During times of heightened anxiety, you need a quick and simple way to cue your calm. The use of three words will begin to quiet the anxious chatter that leads to symptoms. The words are designed to focus you on calm. Three words are easy to access when you get anxious.

The three words may change over time, or you may find you only need one or two words to trigger a calm response. They are not written in stone; if you need to change them, you can. With practice, the words will become your first response to anxiety, and over time, you won't need reminders. When you begin using the three words in place of the automatic anxious words, don't expect to have them at your fingertips. Memorize the words, and keep them written down nearby.

Often, we use danger phrases when we begin to feel anxious, triggering more anxiety. What we tell ourselves makes a difference. Phrases such as, "Uh-oh," or, "This will never end," will trigger that anxious part to be on alert, communicating to your body that you need to be protected from danger. Using the three words replaces the danger phrases with calming affirmation.

When in a state of anxiety or panic, the anxious mind starts to spin uncontrollably. It is in overdrive, trying to find a way out. Your job in recovery is to provide calm. Focusing on the three words will start producing calm. Repeat your three words as many times as you need to bring your anxiety level down. Practice your three words when you are not anxious so they are available to you when you most need them.

Exercise

How do you pick three words? Anxiety affects us physically, cognitively, and emotionally. Choose a word for each category. The words can be a two-word phrase, but not longer. Identify words that will promote calm for each physical, cognitive, and emotional reaction. Memorize these words or write them in your phone, on your hand, on a piece of paper on your nightstand, or on the mirror—wherever you need them most.

Three-word samples:
- Breathe, focus, slow
- Breathe, safe, let go
- Stop, focus, drop
- Quiet, safe, count

Each word has a special meaning and needs to be chosen to counteract the anxious reaction. Using *drop* means drop the shoulders; the word *focus* directs attention to a single item; *quiet* is a signal to quiet the mind. One person used the word *shush*. As long as the words make sense to you and have no negative attachments, they work.

Words like *calm* or *relax* are hard to define in the moment of anxiety and are not recommended. Be specific.

When you start using three words to calm down, let your support people know these words so they can remind you if you get anxious. Support people often share they don't know what to do to help and resort to saying, "Just relax." If you could relax, you would.

With practice, the three words will become part of your calm foundation.

Danny's Resolution

Danny practiced being in the moment without constantly racing forward. Danny wanted answers, and he wanted them yesterday. Danny needed to learn to be quiet so he could listen to the answers he already possessed. "Can't you just tell me the answers? I can pay extra," laughed Danny. It took some time for him to be able to sit quietly for more than a few minutes, so it was recommended he start with two minutes and increase as he felt more comfortable.

Using three words became a powerful skill for Danny. He chose *slow* as the first word. "I decided to use *slow* and *whoa* because I feel like I'm a racehorse. The words rhymed and made me laugh when I heard it. *Whoa* tells me to pull back the reins."

Danny used the three words, breathing, and focus exercises. Danny reported, "My day starts in hectic mode and continues that way. I never stayed grounded and wanted to work on that. I set a timer for five minutes each hour, put the phone down, practiced deep breathing, and refocused. It worked; I actually slowed down and was able to get more work done. And my worries became quiet. One of my coworkers noticed. 'Where is the other Danny?'"

Summary

Practicing three words is something I found accidentally in my recovery. I wrote the words on my hand

and read them whenever I felt anxious to prevent the avalanche of symptoms. My words were *breathe*, *slow*, and *ok*. When my instinct was to run, the words created calm. It took time to trust that anything other than "Let's get out of here" would work. Using the three words requires practice so they become integrated and available when needed. Using three calm words moves the anxious mind toward calm, stopping anxiety in its path. The three words help build the bridge from anxiety to calm.

Calm Affirmation

I can calm myself anytime with words and calm skills. I choose words that will help promote calm and inner peace. My words are...

Chapter 11
The Cycle of Anxiety

Renata's Story

Renata was in a frantic state when we first met. She had been having panic attacks multiple times a week along with high levels of generalized anxiety. Renata found herself looking for anxiety even when she was calm.

Her anxiety antenna was working overtime, leaving Renata feeling off-balance and on high alert. Unable to pinpoint what her anxiety was attached to, she became increasingly anxious due to the unknown. Renata said, "I've never been anxious like this in my life. I don't know where this is coming from, but I feel like I'm in quicksand!"

Renata, a forty-three-year-old mother of two school-aged children, had a panic attack one day after dropping her kids off at school. The panic started as she drove away from school, and it got so bad, she pulled over and called her husband to come get her. "Dave had a client with him in the car, and when they pulled up, I had started to calm down, but I was so humiliated in front of my husband's work client I burst into tears. He was understanding, but I couldn't get over how awful it felt."

Renata was always a little apprehensive when her kids got out of the car for school, thinking it was a normal mom worry, even laughing at herself at times. As her anxiety increased, she began having her mother ride along with her.

Some days, anxiety was so loud she felt unable to drive, so her husband drove the kids. Her anxiety was always worse in the morning, and by the afternoon, she could pick the kids up with little anxiety. "Other mothers drive their kids every day and don't sit in their bedroom scared and panicky; I feel ridiculous."

Renata was embarrassed to admit she had been to the emergency room and urgent care clinics eight times in the last few months. All her medical tests were negative, and she got a clean bill of health each time. The doctors told her it was the stress of having young kids and working, which left her feeling dismissed. The doctor was correct that Renata was under stress, but this wasn't just stress; it was anxiety. Anxiety is about the sense or belief that you are in danger when you are not, that you are not safe in your own body. Stress does not feel like danger and doesn't create a cycle of dread and more fear.

They recommended medication to calm her down, which she chose not to try. After each medical clearance, Renata felt a moment of relief, but within days, the fears started again, and she would cycle back to the emergency room. Anxious thoughts reoccurred: "What if I have another panic attack, and the kids are in the car, and I have to pull over, and it never goes away, and I am stuck with the kids in the car on the side of the road?"

Renata became hyperfocused on any bodily sensation and was convinced the next panic was around the corner. "Weekends used to be easier, and I could calm down. Now, weekends are clouded with anxious thoughts. I have even considered that the doctors are wrong, or my illness is so rare, they don't know what it is yet. I wish they would find something and give me a cure."

Renata laughed. "I have spent enough money at the medical clinics and ER to have my own medical wing." Renata managed to hang on to her humor, but anxious worries were escalating. She was missing work and now at risk of losing her job. Her constant worry was creating fatigue, which created more anxiety about her ability to safely drive her kids. She tried to use willpower and ignore the nagging thoughts but felt overrun by doubts as her anxious imagination ran amok. She bit her lip so hard trying to ignore her thoughts, she ended up in the ER for stitches. When she was alone in the car, she constantly looked in the rearview mirror for her anxiety, even though she admitted she didn't truly believe her anxiety was in the rearview mirror.

"When I get anxious, I can't think straight; all I can do is try to get away from it. My mind becomes filled with fear and worry. It doesn't feel like it's me. I get disoriented, can't problem-solve, and want to run back home. Anxiety takes over in an instant, and then all I can think about is what happens if I panic. Why won't this go away and let me be like everyone else? I feel like I'm a freak."

Skill

Anxiety's job is to protect you from actual dangers and help you seek safety. It is not for manufacturing fears and generating more what-ifs, leading to more anxiety.

Anxiety follows a cycle you can track. It may start with an "uh-oh," shallow breathing, or the urge to run. The first anxious symptom ignites your anxious part to believe there is danger. When the anxious part is awake, it is on alert and starts flooding you with more symptoms, and the cycle of anxiety continues.

Every anxious symptom has a calm replacement. Writing out your anxiety symptoms and calm replacements is a powerful tool. When you experience an anxious symptom, focusing on the calm replacement interrupts the anxious cycle. Anxiety is the problem, and calm is always the solution.

As you identify the steps in the cycle of your anxiety it will give you a sense of control and manageability. It will be clear that your anxiety doesn't come out of the blue, although at times it seems to. The anxious cycle can happen quickly or build over time as you move from anxious thought to anxious thought to anxious thought.

Exercise

There are samples at the end of the exercise.

Draw the "Anxious Me" cycle and add the title on top of the page.

1. Draw a circle; think of it as a clock.
2. Label the first circle "Anxious Me."
3. Create a list of all your anxious symptoms in the order you experience them.
4. Write on the circle starting at twelve o'clock.
5. Go back to the awareness exercise in chapter six if you need to.
6. Continue adding symptoms clockwise until you get to the last symptom.
7. This process helps to look at your anxiety in slow motion.

Draw the "Calm Me" cycle on a second circle with the title on top of the page.

1. Draw a circle; think of it as a clock.
2. Label this "Calm Me."
3. For each anxious symptom, what is its calm response?
4. Write the calm response that would best defuse the charge of the anxious symptom.
5. Continue until there is a calm response for each anxious symptom.

6. If you are not sure of the calm response, leave a blank space to fill in later.
7. Every anxious symptom has a calm response.
8. Your calm skills will grow as you recover.
9. Visualize what it is like to live in a calm cycle.

Draw a third circle titled "Anxious Me and Calm Me" at the top of the page.

1. This is the Anxious Me/Calm Me circle combined.
2. Use two different colored pens.
3. Enter the Anxious Me symptoms on the circle.
4. Enter the Calm Me responses underneath in a different color.
5. Continue doing this for each anxious symptom and its calm response around the circle.

The "Calm Me" tool will help you to break the anxious cycle and infuse calm wherever you are. There is no need to be a victim of your anxiety. The cycles are a powerful visual tool.

As you complete matching the calm responses in the circle, it will become evident that this is a way to quiet anxiety, because it is impossible to be anxious and calm at the same time. Replace each anxious symptom with its calm response.

The calmer you are, the less anxiety will dominate the situation. Focus on practicing calm skills. The more you practice, the more freedom you create in life.

The cycles presented below are examples. Make sure you find your cycle and pattern.

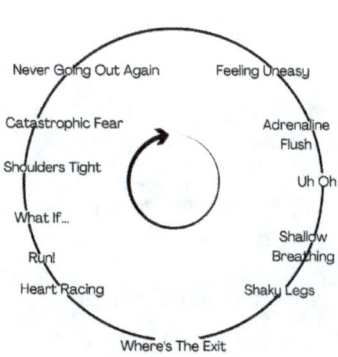

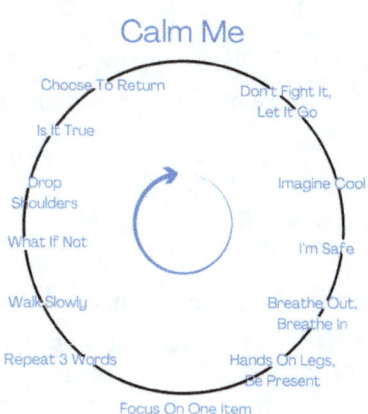

Cycle of Anxiety

Below is another example of the "Anxious Me" cycle combined with the "Calm Me" cycle.

Anxious Me: Oh, here it comes.
Calm Me: Aware of worry, not fueling it.

Anxious Me: What if the worst happens?
Calm Me: What if it does not?

Anxious Me: Feeling overwhelmed.
Calm Me: Thank you. Repeat three words.

Anxious Me: Concerned about breathing.
Calm Me: Breathe out and slow breathing down.

Anxious Me: Have to run.
Calm Me: Walk slowly.

Anxious Me: Confusion about what to do.
Calm Me: Focus on your hand.

Anxious Me: Disconnected feeling.
Calm Me: Hand on heart.

Anxious Me: Stomach tight.
Calm Me: Release the stomach.

Anxious Me: This will never go away.
Calm Me: It always goes away.

Renata's Resolution

One of the biggest blocks for Renata was not understanding what was happening in her body. She didn't understand what caused her anxiety and panic to be so severe. "I felt like I was running from a ghost, but the ghost is inside of me, and I could never run fast enough." Understanding the Cycle of Anxiety was a powerful tool for Renata. She saw where anxiety started, what was maintaining it, and that it was not an "external evil, dark force."

Renata struggled with identifying how she contributed to maintaining her anxious cycle. Until she understood the cycle, it was difficult to break it. "Seeing the cycle helped me pinpoint what was going on inside, and for the first time, I didn't feel so out of control. I realized that my avoidance was leaving room for more anxiety and more worry. Now I can break the cycle. Sometimes it still runs its course, but I don't feel under anxiety's spell."

Renata's recovery was designed around four skills: breathwork, focus exercises, connecting with her heart to stay grounded, and three calming words. The cycle gave her the knowledge she needed to start trusting herself. Renata tracked her wins, and it became a pleasant game for her. When a symptom began, instead of running from it, she repeated her words, put her hand on her heart, and took calm breaths. She needed to turn off the anxious valve that was flooding her with adrenaline and turn on her calm part. That allowed her physical body to calm down, and she started to gain self-confidence. As her confidence grew, she began reclaiming her life and applied rational, logical thinking when she needed to quiet her what-if thoughts.

Summary

The tendency to hide our anxiety creates more anxiety. It creates self-blame and insecurities, adding to the anxious struggle. You didn't cause your anxiety. It is the lack of understanding and fear of anxious symptoms that feeds it. When anxiety is hidden in the shadows, there is no way to address it or change it. Pretending it doesn't exist or ignoring it won't make it disappear.

You can start to dismantle the anxious cycle by increasing awareness of anxiety and how you travel through the cycle. As you learn to step back from anxiety, rather than being consumed by it, you will learn to problem-solve and calm down.

When you are lost in a sea of anxiety, you can only see what is right in front of you. You want to find the quickest way to stop the anxiety at any cost. As you dissect the anxious cycle, you can stand back with objectivity and identify ways to unhook from the cycle.

Anxious thoughts create anxiety-based concerns. The anxious mind is a one-track thinker and will always answer with more anxiety. The calm mind will look for calm solutions to anxiety. No matter how painful anxiety is, it has become part of how you function, and it is hard to let go of it without an alternative to hang on to. Calm is that alternative.

Calm Affirmation

My anxious cycle is a guide. I am breaking the cycle. I know what I need to be calmer every day. I am not the victim; I am the student.

Chapter 12
Panic Attack, Oh No!

The first and most important action to take when you are anxious is to slow the breath. Shallow or hyper breathing promotes anxiety. Deep, slow breaths promote calmness.

Susie's Story

Susie and I had been working on her generalized anxiety for a month when I got a frantic call from her. It was 2:00 p.m., and she was hiding in a building stairway. She was scheduled to do a presentation at a meeting in thirty minutes. Presentations were not an issue for her; she was comfortable in front of an audience. When she called me, the elevator was the problem.

She stepped into the elevator, and as the door closed, she immediately felt a burning in her stomach, which moved up to her chest and throat. She began to breathe shallowly, and her chest felt tight. Her automatic thought was, "I'm having a panic attack. I have to get out of here." She became aware of tingling in her hands, had difficulty focusing, and had an increasing desire to flee. Susie reached forward and pushed the emergency stop button, which sounded an alarm in the elevator, and told me, "I heard the alarm and just froze. I literally felt paralyzed. I could not move. I could not think. I just wanted to flee!"

The elevator door opened, security guards and other passengers were standing in front of her, and all she could do was apologize and head for the exit. The closest exit was the staircase, and that was where she landed when she called me.

Feeling frozen, she believed she was unable to go back to take the elevator to the sixth floor and unable to leave the stairway. Susie collected herself enough to let her group know the presentation would be pushed back thirty minutes, although she didn't have any idea how she would get out of the stairway. It had been about fifteen years since Susie's last panic attack, so it caught her off guard. When I answered the phone, she started to cry and tried to explain what was happening. "Why is this happening now; what did I do wrong?"

Susie's breath was shallow, and she was clenching her jaw and hands. As she slowed and deepened her breaths, she released the tightness in her jaw and hands. This allowed her to start to feel more in control. "Why is this happening now? What did I do?" It was important to keep her focused on calming skills at that moment.

Susie needed to breathe slowly, inhaling a little more each time, allowing her body to return to its normal, natural breathing pattern. Keeping it simple is important in the midst of panic. She could be aware of "why" thoughts without chasing those thoughts. The answer would not make a difference or help her leave the staircase. Susie began to feel calmer and more centered. She found comfort in keeping her hand on her heart, remaining grounded as the desire to flee began to dissipate.

She was able to pull out of the panic, leave the stairway, complete her presentation, and go home. She took the stairs after the meeting, knowing she was avoiding the elevator.

"Would avoidance increase my anxiety?" She agreed it was more important to be gentle with herself and allow permission to do whatever she needed so she could finish her day. It was important for Susie to acknowledge her wins such as reaching out for help, calming down, returning to the meeting, and giving her presentation. She tended to believe struggles outweighed any wins.

We spent time reframing her struggle as an opportunity for growth and learning. Once her panic had passed, the "why" question could be reexamined. It was important for Susie to avoid beating herself up about what happened. She said she would try, but she didn't expect to be successful.

Skill

WHY? WHY? WHY?

"Why am I having panic attacks, and how do I make them disappear?"

"What do I do when I have panic attacks?"

"They will never go away; it's all my fault."

Panic attacks are so gut-wrenchingly scary that it is normal to want to get rid of them as fast as possible. "What do I do? Just tell me what to do!"

The first thing to do is do nothing except breathe. Most people don't like this response to that question. Breathe out. Breathe in slowly. When you get your breath under control, you are on your way out. Your breath is always your first line of defense. You will calm down by breathing.

Managing panic is a process of letting go. It feels counterintuitive; holding on feels like it gives you control. This is not an easy lesson and will require practice. It is your first step. If you have learned to react to panic with more panic, you can learn to let go with calm techniques.

If you have panic attacks, you know how difficult they are to sit with. Every cell in your body is screaming to flee, fight, or freeze! You need to be the voice that says, "Thank you, and I am focused on calm breathing." You cannot calm a screaming, terrified child by screaming louder.

The following steps will help you out of a panic attack. Practice these often so when a panic attack comes, you are ready.

1. Slowly breathe out, breathe in, breathe out, breathe in.
2. Focus on your breath; imagine breathing out panic and breathing in calm.
3. Get grounded.
4. Stay focused on being in your body.

5. Touch your shoulder, put your hand on your knee, and put a hand over your heart or stomach.
6. Focus on a single item, and keep your eyes focused on that item.
7. Ride out the panic.
8. Stay with yourself, breathing out and in.
9. Don't make any decisions. Don't add fear statements such as, "I'm never going here again," or, "I'll never leave home."
10. Do not negotiate with panic; you won't win. You will set yourself up for the next panic attack or anxious reaction.
11. Stay in the present moment.
12. Calm is in you. Remain in your body.
13. Tell your scared self, "This is fear; you have had this before, and it always passes."
14. Breathe out; breathe in.

In a panic, your body feels unsafe. With calm practice, you will feel safe in your body. If you allow the panic symptoms to flow through you, you will learn that panic goes away more quickly, and panic always ends. It is the reaction to it that keeps it fueled.

Panic will come and go on its own if you let it. Letting go of it is the thorny part, because the symptoms are scary, so you may try to escape, make deals, avoid, or fight. These are anxious reactions and don't help. You cannot outrun a panic attack; it will run with you, and when you fight it, you are fighting yourself.

You don't have to run or fight. You know running and fighting do not work. What you must learn to do is to sit with discomfort and breathe. You don't have to like it. Never lie to yourself by trying to convince your scared part that the experience isn't scary.

Anxiety has been lying to you, so don't add to it by lying to yourself that anxiety isn't scary. This is all about fear, but fear is a liar. Anxiety is uncomfortable, disconcerting, and terrifying, but not dangerous.

Once you realize you are safe, even while in the middle of a panic attack, your body will return to a calmer state more quickly. It is your job to tell your body you are safe. You will get in the way if you add scary what-if thoughts. You keep anxiety and panic going full force when you start running toward the exit, tell yourself you are frozen, or hold your breath. The way out of panic is to get control of your breathing and be in touch with your body.

Exercise: Describing Your Panic

(If you don't have panic attacks, you can skip this exercise.)

- When was your earliest memory of a panic attack?
- Describe your symptoms.
- What do you remember about it?
- What did you tell yourself the first time you had a panic attack?
- What decisions or deals did you make?
- How often do you have panic attacks?
- Do you avoid places because of panic?
- What has helped in stopping panic?
- Have you shared your story?

Susie's Resolution

Susie remembered that as a child, she had a panic attack in an elevator. When she was ten, she broke her leg and was on crutches. She was on her way to the doctor for a checkup and was stepping into the elevator. The crutch got stuck in the elevator door, and as the door bounced open and shut, she was convinced it would crush her. Her father was able to lift her into the elevator, and she recalls wanting him to carry her out when they left the building. Her parents joked, "Daddy the donkey-man," and did not realize she was terrified. She was too embarrassed to tell them how it felt and laughed along with them.

As Susie was standing at the elevator door thinking about her presentation, part of her mind wandered back to the crutch stuck in the door and how scared she was. This was what retriggered her old panic. It caught her off guard, and she didn't think to ground herself in the present or breathe through the panic. Susie immediately reacted with more fear and panic.

"This panic attack came one month after my father died. I wasn't consciously thinking about the elevator and crutch because I was focused on my presentation. At that time, I was aware I wanted someone to carry me out of the elevator."

Susie has been practicing her calm skills and breathing to prepare in case she was caught off guard by her anxiety again. It solidified for her that she does have the skills to bring herself back to calm. She also scheduled time to practice being calm while riding an elevator. She has since been panic-free and able to successfully take elevators as needed.

Summary

A wise client described his panic attacks this way: "I'm stuck in my car, and the doors are locked, and the car is on fire, slowly slipping down the side of a cliff, and I can't get out. All logical thinking is trapped with me in the fire."

You can't prevent your mind from bringing up painful memories. At times, it will catch you off guard. Once you have mastered the ability to calm yourself through breathing and calm skills, you will allow your anxiety and panic to float by. You won't need to worry about controlling everything when you know how to invite calm.

In the beginning, it may seem uncomfortable to allow the panic to run its course. It takes a leap of faith to try something different. You already know what you have done in the past isn't working. The first time you let the panic ride will be the hardest. Panic attacks don't last forever. What keeps panic high is adding more fuel in the form of future worry, disordered breathing, and keeping the body tense. Practicing calm instead of practicing anxiety is the key to returning to your calm self.

Calm Affirmation

My panic is scary, and I know I will survive it. I will remain calm and centered and let it flow through me. I am safe.

Chapter 13
Tracking Wins and Struggles

> Instead of "what if-ing" the worst and scariest outcome, what if we imagine the best and most wonderful outcome.
> We can choose our perspective.
> ~Barbara Spaulding, LCSW

Mike's Story

"I have a hard time accepting all my anxiety. I would rather hide from it, wait until it passes, and make it disappear. I feel a lot of anger that I have anxiety." Mike carried a fear about having a fast heartbeat and brain fog when he got anxious. He struggled to stay grounded and present and was constantly looking for a way out.

Mike attended the six-week anxiety relief group and was always a willing participant. He asked questions, shared his anxious struggles, offered support to others, and completed exercises, yet was reluctant to share any of his wins. When asked, Mike replied, "My wins are so insignificant, I feel silly talking about my wins; they don't really matter."

Skill

Tracking your wins and struggles helps you move toward recovery. Small wins are building blocks. Every effort and incremental step toward calm is how recovery grows. Wins offer encouragement, confidence, and empowerment. If you are anxious, I'm guessing you are also self-critical, so tracking your wins gives you an opportunity to practice being your own cheerleader.

You may agree that tracking wins can help you in your recovery journey, but maybe you wonder how what seems like the opposite—tracking your struggles—can help. The answer is that struggles are part of recovery and part of personal growth. You can learn from your struggles. If you pay attention to your struggles, you will see patterns and areas where you consistently get stuck. Keeping a record of your struggles gives you a picture of what skills need more practice. It is a tool used for learning, not judgment. It is possible that one of the skills isn't quite the right fit for you. "When I got anxious, three words were more than I could remember. At times, I was so overwhelmed, I couldn't find the words on my phone. One word worked for me. *Stop* was my word. *Stop* literally quieted the anxiety and gave me time to breathe, slow down, and refocus." I learned this by tracking my struggles.

If there is an area where you aren't progressing, tracking your struggles and your wins offers immediate feedback on what is working and what skill needs to be adjusted. Recovery is a process. It is neither a straight line nor is it magic. It is work, which requires patience and sometimes adjustments. Tracking gives you the feedback to make those adjustments.

Struggling means you are in the game of recovery. Tracking struggles and wins allows you to fully engage with recovery, the ups, the downs, and your successes. If you can acknowledge what is true without judgment and criticism, you can move forward. Building a bridge from anxiety to calm is simply one foot in front of the other.

Exercise

Create two charts, one for struggles and one for wins, like the following:

DATE	STRUGGLES	
	DESCRIPTION	LESSON

DATE	WINS	
	DESCRIPTION	LESSON

Mike's Resolution

Mike was aware he was responding to an old family tape about not tooting his own horn: "Be humble; be modest; don't brag." That was the message. The group encouraged Mike to let go of that old message and be proud of his wins. He said, "I am getting better at giving myself credit. I have been using the struggles and wins charts. It still feels easier to keep track of the struggles, but I see the benefit and am starting to be proud of my wins, even if it is just in this group. My buddies would never get it."

As Mike got more comfortable with his progress, he began to acknowledge his wins and appreciate his struggles as he put his foundation of calm in place.

Summary

Tracking wins gives you credit along the way to see even the smallest of steps as you progress. You need wins to counter the negativity and despair that comes with anxiety. Building a new, calm foundation is created by connecting and practicing calm skills, so over time, you will be more familiar and likely to seek the calm path, not the anxious path.

Everyone progresses in their own time frame; respect yours and your pace. There is nothing to be gained by comparing yourself to others. Be patient; this isn't a race. Learning to be calm may seem like a new skill; however, being calm is a part of you that has simply been sleeping.

Calm Affirmation

I accept my wins and struggles. "Calm me" accepts and stays grounded. My feelings are not my enemy; they are my teachers. I love and care for all parts of myself.

Chapter 14
Defining Your Recovery

Every day is a new day. If you wake up and your brain is already on the "anxious train" try getting on a "calm train." Redirect your thoughts, tell yourself you ARE safe, breathe out!

Kathy's Story

Seventy-three-year-old Kathy was a reluctant group member. She believed she had tried everything without any long-term success. Her daughter attended a few of my talks and convinced Kathy to try one more time, so she joined one of the anxiety relief groups. Kathy openly shared, "I have many doubts and fears that this program or any program can help me anymore. I have tried everything and even considered the cabbage soup diet. I was desperate when I was younger, and I just don't want to be disappointed again."

Kathy wasn't alone in her skepticism about yet another anxiety program. Most people have tried to overcome their anxiety, and it is natural to have doubts. Kathy was frustrated and sad that she was still in a battle with her anxiety after fifty years. She had struggled with bouts of agoraphobia, often unable to leave her home for months at a time. She was embarrassed, resigned, and, to her surprise, angry.

"I grew up on a farm in an era where kids didn't speak up, and in my family, this was especially true for girls. I still remember my father saying girls need to be quiet unless asked, and he never asked. Mother was too shy to talk back and warned us not to ask too many questions around my father. I think we were all a little scared of his temper. All the families I knew were like that. You just accepted it."

Her present family was often in crisis. "Too much drama for an old lady like me; sometimes I use anxiety as an excuse to stay away." She was honest that she didn't want to spend a lot of time with her family. "Lately, I prefer the company of my feline pets. Short visits with my adult kids are all I can stand lately."

Skill

Living with anxiety means life is about managing and avoiding anxious feelings. What-if worries can become an all-consuming, exhausting job. While the focus is on feeling less anxious, the cost is alarmingly high. Avoiding anxiety means restricting freedoms such as daily activities and social events. It becomes harder to recognize your own life.

People have shared:

"I used to drive everywhere; now I can't drive down the street without getting anxious."

"I was always up for a weekend away; now I don't leave my house."

"I never missed work, and this year, I had to resign because of my anxiety."

The list of ways anxiety impacts and restricts life can feel endless. Anxiety recovery allows you to take your life back.

In the beginning of the program, most people have a hard time connecting to the idea that they can be successful at having an anxiety-free life. If you are living with anxiety, the view is filtered through an anxious lens, and life always looks anxious. As you look more and more through a calm lens, your life will begin to change.

Life without anxiety will require many changes. Recovery may mean identifying unhealthy or codependent relationships, ending people-pleasing, rejecting perfectionism, leaving toxic workplaces, and improving self-care. This is your recovery. You define how you change your life and recover.

Maintaining calm includes discovering and speaking your truth. If you don't, anxiety will be that voice for you. Recovery doesn't work if you take care of others' needs and ignore your own. Everyone's recovery is different, and as anxiety starts to quiet, it becomes possible to identify what you truly want and don't want.

Exercise: Life without Anxiety

Your goal in recovery is to create a life without anxiety. If anxiety has been restricting you from parts of your life, this is the time to start bringing back what you have lost or have become afraid of. You must think of yourself as more than "just about anxiety." Thinking beyond anxiety will help support and build your next phase, one of calm. At first, it may be hard to imagine being anxiety-free. As you learn more calm skills, it is vital to look toward a new way of being. Imagining a calm life will support your recovery.

Think beyond anxiety recovery to the other things you would want in your life.

- I want more of...
- I want less of...
- I need to speak up about...
- I need to tell the truth about...
- What activities, hobbies, people, personal growth, or travel would you look forward to?
- Add any areas that are important to you.
- What are the blocks that might get in the way?

Leave a few blank spaces here to add to the list as you recover.

Kathy's Resolution

The group helped Kathy define her own recovery. She liked the idea that she could make her own decisions. She felt she had such little control while in her anxious days. She decided her family's issues were not hers to take on because she needed her energy for her recovery, so she started setting boundaries.

Once she gave herself the freedom to speak up, she was very clear about what she wanted. "I think my family was surprised—no, shocked—when I started to speak up. I was a little surprised also, but it felt so good," shared Kathy.

Kathy was clear about what she wanted. It was important to her to feel less anxious while at home, be able to invite friends for coffee, and run a few errands. Her recovery was her personal design. It was the beginning of feeling empowered. One group session, she excitedly shared, "I started volunteering at my local hospice, something I always thought I would do after retiring from nursing. It has been so fulfilling. There's just not room in my life today for anxiety." Everyone cheered.

Kathy saw she needed better boundaries with her grown children. "My anxiety got in the way of parenting. I know I leaned on my kids when I felt unable to function, and now that has changed. I can allow my grown children their opinions as I find my own voice again." As she recovered, her kids started to get along better when they visited.

"What was the most helpful for me was creating my three words. In my anxious days, I added to my worries with more worries and more anxious thoughts. The words gave me an alternative, and I think anyone who knows me also knows my words. My granddaughter sent me a birthday card and said she was proud of me, and she used my words to calm down during a math test. It was an honor to share that with her. I hate that my grandbaby has anxiety, and I hope I can continue to be a source of calm for her."

Kathy practiced letting go of people-pleasing and accepted her anxiety as a partner rather than the monster she previously thought it was. As she became more confident, she requested family sessions, and so her family began their journey of healing.

Summary

It is crucial that your recovery from anxiety be yours. When you are in the throes of anxiety, you slowly lose your voice. Recovery isn't just about freedom from symptoms, but it is also about reclaiming your life. You can do that by listening to what the heart wants and what you need. Continue strengthening boundaries, setting limits, and respecting yourself. Many anxious people give up on their needs because anxiety makes them feel inadequate and unworthy. Recovery is about working toward wholeness as you move toward calm. Everyone learns in their own way; the lessons and exercises are for you to work with. Make this recovery yours; claim it, and own it.

Calm Affirmation

I am the only me, unique and valuable. I am learning to honor and listen to my inner voice.

Chapter 15
Calm Lens vs. Anxious Lens

> **Which lens?**
> When you look through activities and events through your anxious lens, you will produce anxiety. Try and see the same activities or events through a calm, relaxed lens. How does that look different? Practice the calm lens.

Caroline's Story

Almost everyone on the planet feels stress about going to the dentist. Stressed or not, people manage to get in the dentist chair—except Caroline. Caroline was not only stressed, she was also paralyzed, and because she had been unable to go to the dentist for years, she now needed emergency dental work. This happened at a point when she was already working with me and learning skills to reduce anxiety.

As a child, Caroline needed extensive dental work. It was expensive, and her parents complained about the cost. Caroline heard her parents arguing, and she felt responsible for their eventual divorce. It was not her fault, but as a child, she believed it was. Additionally, she developed a fear of going to the dentist she could not shake as an adult.

She viewed going to the dentist through her anxious lens. Caroline listed all her fears. "My biggest fear is being trapped in the dentist's chair. If I feel trapped, I'm afraid of having anxiety and needing to scream for help. I am also scared that I would be so overwhelmed I would flee, regardless of what apparatus is in my mouth. Then I would be too embarrassed to return." The anxious lens had convinced her she might have a panic attack or suffocate in the middle of dental work.

As Caroline talked through her fears, she was beginning to see the logic that had been missing. We first questioned each fear to assess whether it would hold up.

Was Caroline truly trapped? No.

Was she likely to run out of the room with dentist's equipment in her mouth? No.

Could she imagine herself screaming in the middle of the visit? No.

Would the dentist let her suffocate? No.

Could she ask the dentist for help? Yes.

Each answer gave her relief and built confidence. She decided if she needed to scream, she would do so after the appointment.

Viewing the situation through an anxious lens does not allow for logic, and it cannot problem-solve. After addressing her fears, we used the problem-solving skill.

If she needed to go to the bathroom, she was sure the dentist would encourage her to go.

If she was having difficulty breathing or any discomfort, the dentist would stop the treatment and not let her suffocate. She laughed and said, "Suffocating patients probably wouldn't be good for his business."

She said she could not imagine running out of the office with his equipment, partly because "there's no way I can run on these old knees."

The anxious mind offers scary outcomes. The more Caroline questioned the validity of her fears, the lighter she became until we were both laughing at some of the imagined images. She started to see that the fear of being trapped isn't the same as actually being trapped. Caroline needed a different image, and she learned to look through a calm lens to create a new image to hold in her mind.

Skill

We are using the word *lens* to illustrate the way one views a situation.

When you are living with anxiety, you view life through an anxious lens. Thoughts consist of what-ifs, fears, and rumination. Physically, you hold your breath, tense your muscles, and create a negative anxious loop. The anxious lens does not let any other ideas or possibilities in and is closed, dark, and scary. Everything you see contained in the anxious space ends up producing more anxiety.

A calm lens is the opposite of an anxious lens. When you live calmly, you see possibilities and opportunities. It isn't dark and scary being in your own body. You may feel apprehension, but you don't see danger everywhere. It is easier to problem-solve when you are calm. Recovery is about finding calm, so using a calm lens is a step toward recovery. My anxious lens told me I could get lost in a store and never be found. My calm lens reminded me that instead of getting confused or lost, the better option would be to ask for directions.

Exercise: Anxious Lens

1. Identify a few events or activities you are struggling with due to anxiety or panic.
2. Describe in detail the event through an anxious lens.
3. How will things proceed according to the anxious lens?
4. What might be the outcome?
5. How will you be afterward?

Calm Lens

1. Use the same events and activities as above.
2. Describe in detail the event through a calm lens.
3. How will things proceed according to the calm lens?
4. What might be the outcome?
5. How will you be afterward?

Example: A Drive Through Your Anxious Lens

"I can't drive that far; the expressway is impossible. I get near the car and feel my hands shaking; my breathing is shallow, and I feel sweaty. In the car, I am gripping the wheel, knuckles turning white, and my stomach feels like a knot. I know any minute I may speed down the road or pull over. I will have to wait until nighttime to continue. Or I will have to call my friend to get me, or worse yet, call 911, because by then, I will be having a heart attack. Yeah, I'm not getting in the car."

A Drive Though Your Calm Lens

"My body is relaxed, my breathing pattern is normal, and I'm ok with any discomfort. Driving is relaxing. I have a loose grip on the steering wheel and the windows are open; I'm feeling the wind in my hair, enjoying the scenery, and listening to music. Woohoo!"

Apply this to as many things as you need. The more you practice, the more your brain will get used to shifting from the anxious lens to a calm lens. If you have been anxious, the anxious lens has become the norm. The anxious lens is about avoiding and creating restrictions. The more you practice switching to the calm lens, the more natural calm becomes.

Caroline's Resolution

The calm lens allowed Caroline to identify which skills she could use. Caroline decided the first thing she would do was talk to the dentist about her anxiety and let him know what she needed. She used the calm lens, starting with the ride to the dentist. She imagined herself listening to quiet music, practicing calm breathing, and keeping her focus. She wrote her three words on stickers and stuck them on the car dashboard. "Whenever the anxious lens appeared, I said thank you and switched to the calm lens."

She gave herself permission to be anxious and chose not to fight with herself. She acknowledged that going to the dentist is uncomfortable but not dangerous. Caroline was able to stay relatively calm during the visit, although she still does not enjoy the dentist. Join the crowd.

Summary

You can apply this to as many events as you need. The more you practice switching from an anxious lens to a calm lens, the faster and smoother it becomes.

Right now, you are likely using an anxious lens and need to learn to use your calm lens. If you switch from your anxious lens to a calm lens, you find solutions. At first, the calm lens will be a little rusty; it hasn't been used for a while. "If I have a calm lens, it has been packed in the attic for the last twenty years, and I wouldn't recognize the box it's in." If that's the case, use your imagination and start shifting to the opposite of anxiety. With practice, it becomes easier and more natural to look through your calm lens.

Don't waste time fighting with an anxious lens; accept and use your energy to practice with your calm lens.

Calm Affirmation

I can switch to a calm lens at any moment. My anxious lens is not the only choice, and I choose calm.

Chapter 16
Practice Schedules

It is easy to be discouraged by anxiety. Anxiety is an emotion. React with anxiety, and you get more anxiety. React with calm, and you will get more calm.

Practice, practice calm.

Nicolas's Story

Nicolas had recently experienced a panic attack on a flight for work. He had always been uncomfortable flying, but it was a requirement of his job, and he fought through it, took a sedative, or had a few drinks.

As Nicolas described what happened on the flight, he realized his anxiety started before he got on the plane. He was waiting to board and felt an uneasiness he described as "the ickies." On his way to his seat, he felt tightness in his throat, and once seated, he clenched his jaw. While the plane was ascending, he gripped the seat arms, felt a headache ramping up, and had an unsafe feeling. As the plane leveled out, he began having heart palpitations and was breathing fast. "I didn't know what to do at that point. I tried breathing exercises and got up and walked to the restroom. The symptoms dissipated, so I went back to my seat."

As his anxiety quieted down, he was flooded with the idea of jumping out the window: "I told myself, 'If I get through this flight, I will never fly again.'" He packed his catastrophic fear and the deal he made into the back of his mind and was relieved to get home safely. He did not share what happened with anyone, feeling "silly and childish."

A few months after that anxious flight, he found out he was going to be a grandfather, and his son invited him and his wife to his grandchild's birth across the country. Nicolas was so excited, he momentarily forgot about his anxiety. As he waited for the flight confirmation on the phone, his fears came alive. "It started with, 'What if I get anxious and want to jump out of the plane or run up and down the aisles screaming?'" He was unable to finalize the flight arrangements. Nicolas considered driving and realized it may be easier to get help. When his wife asked about the airline tickets, he shared what had happened. She was understanding and gave him my number.

Nicolas's anxiety had gone from a little uncomfortable to full-blown panic. "I can't let anxiety prevent me from such an incredible experience. I have always been able to manage my anxiety. I do not know what I did to cause this." When I asked, "What do you think you did to cause your anxiety?" Nicolas tried to find an answer. He was surprised the answer was "nothing." He did not cause his anxiety; there was no need for self-blame.

Nicolas needed to understand how his anxiety took hold and what he could do to reduce it. We can only control how we react to anxiety, and his anxiety started with an uncomfortable sensation prior to the flight. He tried to ignore it and suppress his fear and uncomfortable sensations. In the anxious part of his mind, the fear started to grow, and it followed him onto the plane. If he had been able to acknowledge the fear, he may have been able to release it.

We started with general work around his beliefs and mindset. We set up a practice schedule to practice his calm skills. At first, there was no room in his mind for any other outcome besides becoming so anxious that he would want to jump out of the plane. He suspected it was not the plane he wanted to jump out of but rather his body. We used a logical sequence of questions to assess how true his catastrophic fear was:

- Do you have a clear image of how to open a plane window? No.
- Do you have an idea how you would physically get out the window? No.
- Are you likely to break a safety rule? No.
- Is it likely you would be successful jumping out the plane window? No.

His logical-thinking self already knew the answers, but his anxious, scared part was not logical. When he became anxious, he was unable to engage his logical-thinking self.

Nicolas's practice schedule included the skill of saying "thank you" to his anxious thoughts and letting them go. Thanking anxiety is a way of removing any animosity or the need to fight with it.

Nicolas used the anxious-lens-versus-calm-lens skill and replaced his scary flight images with images of himself feeling calm on the plane. He could imagine looking around, talking with his wife, breathing in a relaxed way, loosening his grip on the seat, and unclenching his jaw. He became calm enough to purchase the tickets. It was important that he not fight through or ignore the anxiety and that he bought the tickets only when he felt calm.

Skill

Practice schedules are an important step in recovery. A practice schedule is not about continuing your war and struggling with anxiety. Those methods are more anxious practice, and you have done enough of that. A practice schedule builds your skills in creating a calm foundation.

The practice schedule is built in consecutive, small steps so you have a high chance of success and build confidence and strength in being calm. If a step feels too big, take a step back. It is all about practicing calm over and over.

As you walk through the practice schedule, you will use and solidify all the calm skills you have gained. Recovery is incomplete if you are avoiding things due to anxiety. You set this method and design it, so it doesn't feel frightening. After years of being stuck in anxious mode, many people find the little successes are enjoyable and provide hope that recovery can be reached.

The more you practice being calm, the more the skills will be with you the moment you need them. The practice schedule has to be safe with the minimum chance of triggering overwhelming anxiety. If you do get anxious, move back to an earlier step, only moving forward as you master each step.

It is all about calm practice. To fully recover, you need a lot of calm practice. The anxious body and mind need to become as accustomed to calm as they have previously been to anxiety.

Exercise

Establish time every day to follow through with your practice schedule. The skills you practice will enable you to calmly address the situations in your life that produce anxiety.

Once you have these calm skills in place, you can practice them in the real world.

Pick something you are avoiding and break it down into small steps. Each step should build on the previous step and needs to be closer to what you are avoiding. If you get anxious while doing a step, drop back a step, and do that step until you can do it calmly. No need for concern if you need to step back. Do not skip any steps. Continue doing the steps till you are comfortable doing what you have been avoiding.

Example

My scary situation is to drive thirty miles to my friend's house, including getting on the highway. I have been able to drive to the end of my block.

Steps:

1. Drive to the end of my block, return home.

2. Drive two blocks, return home.
3. Drive four blocks, return home.
4. Drive to highway entrance, return home.
5. Enter the highway and exit at first exit, return home.
6. Enter the highway and drive to the second exit, return home.
7. Enter the highway and drive ten miles, re turn home.
8. Enter the highway and drive to your friend's house. Congratulate yourself on conquering your anxiety-producing situation!

Here are some reasons practice schedules are sometimes unsuccessful:

- You skip a step when you have success. This sets you up for failure.
- You don't give yourself the time needed for each step.
- A step produces anxiety but you keep pushing forward. Instead, go back to the previous step.
- You miss a scheduled practice time. Get back on your schedule.

Practice schedules are about practicing calm, not being tough and pushing through anxiety. This is about learning to create and maintain calm.

Nicolas's Resolution

The confidence Nicolas built during his practice schedule was about knowing he could calm himself down in the face of anxiety. He was able to successfully apply that skill to his fear of flying.

His goal for our work was to calmly return to flying, so we focused on that. Nicolas learned about using three calm words and how to focus his thoughts. We added this skill to his calm practice schedule. He had four weeks before the flight. These were his steps:

1. Talk about his concerns with his wife.
2. Purchase tickets.
3. View photos of planes.
4. Read articles about planes.
5. View videos of planes taking off. This step created a surge of anxiety, and he returned to step four before moving on.
6. Drive to the airport and watch planes take off and land.
7. Enter the airport and watch planes from the gates.

Each time his anxiety crept up he used his skills to calm down. He replaced his fear of needing to jump out any windows with the knowledge that he could sit through discomfort and return to a state of calm.

When Nicolas's anxiety crept back, he stopped and used his three calm words: *breathe*, *safe*, and *focus*. That quieted the flare of anxiety, and his anxiety lessened. Each time the "run" thought occurred, he focused on the image of being with his son. When his anxious mind chattered at him, he said, "Thank you, and I am focused on my family."

Nicolas successfully flew two thousand miles and shared in the birth of his grandchild. He did not have any issues with anxiety. He laughed at his fear of jumping out a window when he realized how small the windows were. "It is hard to conceive how I ever thought I would fit."

Nicolas called me after the trip. "I am thrilled I made the trip. I broke down in the hospital with joy and relief. If I had missed my granddaughter's birth, I would have been heartbroken. Maybe it doesn't matter what caused the anxiety or where it came from. I know if it returns, I know what to do." Nicolas's confidence wasn't about flying; it was knowing he could calm himself down in the face of anxiety.

Summary

One of the hardest parts of recovery is the concept of facing anxiety. The idea produces intense resistance, which is rooted in fear. The practiced response to anxiety has been to run, fight, freeze, or avoid, and that old first line of defense has not worked; the way out is to practice calm.

Eventually, recovery will require a return to your "scary" places to know you are truly free. Practicing calm is a less threatening approach to use your calm skills and reduce anxiety. A practice schedule allows you to practice calm skills and identify which skills are solid and which skills need developing.

Your path to recovery will be greatly enhanced by practicing calm consistently. Don't wait until you need to go somewhere where you generally feel anxious to practice calm; this does not build a solid foundation. The idea is for you to take control of your program and create a schedule you can practice—and practice,

practice, practice. If all you can do is take two steps out the door, then do that every day until your anxiety lessens. Your path to recovery is paved with calm practice, which will eventually become second nature.

Continue practicing, knowing you may experience bumps along the way. Be proud of yourself. You are creating your recovery.

Calm Affirmation

I can break down fears into small increments and stay present and grounded in my body. I have calm in me.

Chapter 17
Focus

Janey's Story

Janey was fourteen when she first came for help. She was a high school athlete competing in basketball and field hockey. She loved sports.

Until recently, Janey had been excited about her sports, had friends on the team, and excelled in her classes. Her mother noticed Janey seemed less interested in attending games and became concerned.

Janey finally told her mother that she experienced a panic attack after a game and was afraid she would have more. "I knew what a panic attack was because my cousin had them. I felt out of control while it took over, and I ended up running off the court." After the panic attack, Janey had trouble letting go of the fear that it might come back. Janey tried to distract herself with video games, which cleared her mind while she was playing, but it didn't last. "I can't play video games all day."

The panic was worse because a player from the opposing team saw her "acting strange" and told others. She was terrified of having another attack and calling attention to herself. Middle school is hard enough, and team sports are intense. "I can't be worried about this stupid panic popping up in the middle of a game. I don't want to let my teammates down, and I don't think I can tell them."

When Janey and I met, she shared she has been anxious on and off in her life. "Sports has been my escape where I can burn off the anxious energy, but now even that has been affected." She missed a few practices and started to avoid her teammates. "I make up excuses, but I have to get back, or I will lose my place on the teams." The entire experience was taking a toll on her self-esteem.

The first step was to educate Janey and her family about anxiety and panic. During a family discussion regarding when her anxiety started, Janey shared that her younger brother had leukemia. He had been in remission for four years, but she still worried. "I wonder if one day I'll come home from practice and he will be back in the hospital." Janey had not talked to her parents about her fears, trying to be the perfect daughter. She didn't want anyone to have to worry about her too.

In a family session, her mother shared, "I have tried to stay upbeat and positive for everyone. I imagine that didn't leave room to talk about fears." Her parents realized that with all the care her brother needed, Janey got lost in the shuffle. Her parents attended a few sessions to discuss her brother's illness and how it impacted Janey. She was able to ask questions and her parents listened to her fears.

Janey reframed her description of her anxiety from a "weird medical problem" to a sign that she was emotionally overwhelmed. Once she was able to able to identify her anxiety as a sign of being overloaded, she started to focus her attention by grounding herself in the environment around her.

Skill

Focusing is a way for you to calm your thoughts, fears, and anxieties. Focusing on the environment around you grounds you in the present moment. When you are anxious, you are not in the present moment, but you are dwelling in fears from your past or thinking about future worries. Focusing on the present moment releases you from your anxiety.

When you are in the throes of anxiety, it's natural to use whatever skill you have. The goal when you are anxious is simple: make it go away. It's easy to use distractions; they are everywhere.

You grab the phone, play games, make a call, or read an article—anything to distract you from your symptoms. Distraction provides a temporary sense of control, but it doesn't allow for lasting calm.

Using distractions means always needing to be busy, and when you are quiet, anxiety will be there. That means continuing to be scared about living in your own body, which is exhausting. You are not designed to be anxious all the time.

Calm is always within you and available to you, even if you don't know that yet. Long-term relief will come from the internal knowledge that your calm part is always available. One way to reach your calm is by focusing on something in the present.

The more you focus on the present moment, the less anxious you will become. Focusing and grounding yourself is an invaluable skill in recovering from anxiety.

Exercise: Focus

Start building your ability to focus by using your five senses.

- **Smell:** Pick up a piece of fruit and smell it. Cut it open and smell and notice the difference.
- **Touch:** Pick up a few items. Notice through touch how they are different or similar. Spend a few moments being aware of their different textures, weights, and shapes.
- **Taste:** Use your meals as time to practice focusing. Be aware of tastes and textures. Eat slowly and consciously. Try dried fruit and compare it to fresh fruit. When you eat a meal, slow down, and be aware of how your taste buds are activated.
- **Sight**: If you can go outside, look around and focus on one item. If it's a tree, first look at the entire tree, then a branch, then a leaf.

- A very easy exercise when you are anxious is to simply look at your finger and hold the gaze. Switch to your arm, hand, and then leg until any anxiety has quieted.
- Look at an item's pattern and pick one color or shape to focus on.
- **Hearing:** Listen to a piece of music and listen to each instrument as if it is the only one playing.
    - When outside, focus on a particular sound, such as a bird, car, siren, or talking. Separate it from other sounds.
    - When you watch TV, focus on a particular voice, sound, or background music.
    - Make yourself an audio of calming statements and encouragement. It is soothing to hear your own voice teaching you to focus and be calm.

Self-Talk Focus

When you are anxious in a situation, use your self-talk to become focused. Here are some examples.

- **Work:** I am in a conference room, sitting in a chair, and I feel my feet on the ground. I focus on my breath out and my breath in.
- **Car:** I am in my blue car with white seats. My hands are on the steering wheel, and I see cars on the road. I can feel my body in the seat, and my breath is calm.

- **Party:** I am at a table, sitting in a chair, with my feet on the floor. The table has plastic forks and a centerpiece with yellow daisies.

When you practice focus, the anxious mind will keep chattering. Respond with, "Thank you." Return to focus. Each time your anxious mind interrupts, repeat, "Thank you," and return to focus. It is important to let the anxious mind know you are learning to focus.

Safe Place

Creating safe places in our minds is a way to boost calm. It is not necessary to wait until you are anxious to try it. It is an exercise you can use to put the anxious fire out.

Example:

1. Think of an image where you feel calm and safe. It can be a forest, ocean, mountains, or a place in your home.
2. Imagine the details with all your senses.
3. Draw a picture.
4. Record it.
5. Find a picture of your safe place and print it.
6. Name it.
7. Practice being there in your mind.
8. Breathe into the image.
9. Change and add as you like.

Janey's Resolution

The family sessions helped Janey understand the dynamics of her brother's illness and let go of the burden she carried. The insight and family healing were not enough for her to recover, because anxiety had taken on a life of its own. Janey was able to use the focus exercises, and as she felt calmer, she was able to return to the sports she loved. The rest of the work for Janey was building her calm skills and calm foundation.

One of the symptoms that concerned Janey was depersonalization. It is a common symptom that wakes up the anxious mind. It is defined as feeling disconnected to yourself. "I sometimes feel outside my body and ungrounded, which is very scary." This is unnerving and ungrounding. It becomes a call to wake up your anxious part so it can be on guard at all times, especially when feeling lightheaded or disoriented. Janey was able to use focus exercises to bring herself back to the present moment and into her body.

Janey spent time watching high school basketball and field hockey to practice her focusing skills.

She imagined herself on the court, staying grounded, focused, and calm. She created this focus exercise: "My anxiety reminds me I am alive. My feet are on the ground, my hands are relaxed, and my head is in the game, nowhere else." She practiced her calm dialogues when she wasn't anxious so the calm would be with her when she needed it.

Her ability to focus allowed her to remain calm during the games.

Summary

There is no benefit to letting anxious thoughts spiral. The ability to focus when you are anxious will greatly enhance your ability to calm down.

You are learning the skill of practicing calm in the face of anxiety. It is a skill to have when life feels stressful and you need to concentrate or make decisions. The mind tends to focus on what scares you, and you can learn to redirect your mind with focus exercises.

Calm Affirmation

It is within me to remain focused, grounded, and centered. If I lose focus, I bring it back when I need it.

Chapter 18
Self-Talk

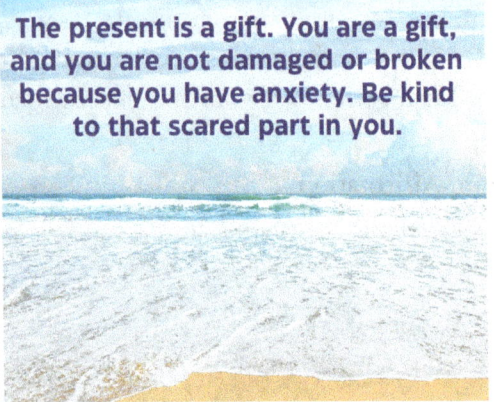

The present is a gift. You are a gift, and you are not damaged or broken because you have anxiety. Be kind to that scared part in you.

Randall's Story

Randall absolutely hated his anxiety, routinely yelling at it and labeling it his wicked twin. He described anxiety as his number one enemy: "I just want it dead and buried." It was painful listening to how critical and punitive he was about his anxiety, and ultimately, about himself. "If I am nice to anxiety or give it an inch, it will suck me down and take over completely. As I say that out loud, I realize it has already taken over. The more I yell, the stronger it gets. I don't see a way out."

It was extremely difficult for Randall to accept the idea that anxiety was not the enemy. Randall started to recognize that his negative self-talk was an adaptation to growing up in a critical and punitive family.

It horrified him when he saw the similarity between how his mother treated him and how he was treating himself.

That realization provided Randall with an opening to consider a different point of view. He had been taught that feelings should be rejected. In his family of five boys, feelings just got in the way. Vulnerability was described as quicksand. His tremendous drive toward perfection and unhealthy competition was emotionally damaging. "There were countless, rigid rules about behavior. I was always afraid to make a mistake. That has carried into my adult life, even for simple things."

When Randall painted his living room, he put eight samples of beige paint on the wall, trying to find the best one. He was so worried that he asked his girlfriend to pick the color. "When she did and we painted it, I was still sure it was the wrong color. And I am talking about beige paint!"

Randall's first assignment was to spend the week being kind and compassionate toward himself, especially if he felt scared. He was visibly uncomfortable with this suggestion, but desperate enough to try. "Maybe you aren't the therapist for me; the idea of self-kindness seems so foreign." He knew he always had the option to go back to his self-hatred. But after one week of being less critical and a trifle kinder, he was softer, less defensive, and open to taking another step. He shared that it had been an emotional week; he'd had random bouts of crying, which, although uncomfortable, left him feeling lighter.

Randall spent time writing to his fears each day while letting his fears write to him. He applied the same writing technique with sadness and anger. The more he wrote and the more he listened, the calmer he felt. "I truly believed if I looked at all this, I would get stuck further in it, but it has been quite the opposite." Randall kept his three calm words inside his journal and used the words if he felt anxious. His three words were *breathe*, *present*, and *safe*.

Skills

Negative self-talk functions as a punitive inner critic. Negative self-talk creates anxiety because you are constantly berating and criticizing yourself. It is hard to function when we barrage ourselves with a steady stream of negative, punitive comments. Negative self-talk is a heavy burden to carry. It is often an integrated message from childhood. When a child is criticized, they learn to criticize and dislike themselves.

Anxiety recovery is about striving to be whole, and being whole is difficult if you keep putting yourself down. People with anxiety are extremely hard on themselves. "I hate myself for having anxiety" is a common expression.

Imagine criticizing a child for being scared or yelling at a child when they make a mistake learning to read. They will feel horrible about themselves, which doesn't help in either scenario. Now apply that to yourself. Feeling horrible about yourself will undermine your progress. Recovery is difficult, and negative self-talk makes it much more strenuous.

How do you change negative self-talk? You start by becoming aware of what is true right now in this moment. Listen to the negativity and the snide comments you make about yourself and develop a kinder approach. Identify your untenable expectations and your struggles with control and perfection. Be aware of comparing yourself to others. Acknowledge your own success and struggles the way you would for a friend.

Exercise: Negative Self-Talk
- What is your earliest memory of negative self-talk?
- Where do you think you learned this form of talk?
- What is the negative talk trying to protect you from?
- How does it hurt you and get in your way?
- Have you found any ways to quiet the talk?
- Are the critical comments true?

Practice rewriting negative self-talk.
1. Identify a negative self-talk statement.
2. Decide if it is true.
3. Rewrite the negative self-talk statement, turning it into a neutral or positive statement.
4. Repeat this process many times.

Your rewrite is based on what is true, not what you have been told or what your inner critic has been saying. You rarely stop and question what you say, even when there is no evidence of truth.

Here are some rewrite examples:

- Negative self-talk says, "I am not a good student; therefore, I am too dumb to try to get into school."
- Rewrite: "I never learned how to study when I was young, but now I am an adult, and I learn all the time."
- Negative self-talk says, "You were never as good as your sister."
- Rewrite: "I was always as good as my sister; I am different and unique."
- Negative self-talk says, "I am not good enough to accomplish that."
- Rewrite: "I will learn as I go and figure out how to accomplish that."

What can you do to use positive self-talk? What would get in the way of making that shift?

Words Can Hurt Your Recovery

A few changes in how you talk to yourself can impact behavior.

1. Using the word *can't* closes all the doors completely. If you say you can't, you believe it is not possible.
2. Often, the word *can't* is a stand-in for, "I'm scared." The statement "I can't go to the party," is really, "I am scared to go." Practice changing the word *can't* to what is true.
   - Example: "I can't attend the outing."
   - Change to: "I am scared and acknowledge my fear so I can identify a calm skill to help me."

3. Add the word *yet* at the end of the sentence. List a few things you believe to be in your "can't" category and add the word. Notice the difference.
   - Example: "I can't drive to the chiropractor."
   - Change to: "I can't drive to the chiropractor *yet*."
   - Example: "I don't know how to recover."
   - Change to: "I don't know how to recover *yet*."

4. The word *but* is another word that shuts the door. Using *and* makes it neutral.
   - Example: "I did my practice, *but* I got anxious."
   - Change to: "I did my practice, *and* I got anxious."
   - Example: "I drove ten minutes today *but* got anxious."
   - Change to: "I drove ten minutes today *and* got anxious."

5. Using "thank you" is a great way to acknowledge anxiety without fighting it.
   - Example: "It's too hard to practice being calm. My mind keeps chattering. Yak, yak, yak."
   - Response: "Thank you, and right now, I am focusing on calm."
   - Example: "But I have to worry."
   - Response: "Thank you, and I am going to practice my calm skills."

Being present is part of recovery. It is common when you get upset to say, "You will be ok." If you scrape a knee, it makes sense; it will heal. It doesn't work as well with anxiety. Giving anxiety the idea that you will be "ok" in the future invites anxiety to wait until that happens. You may be uncomfortable, and you are also ok.

Randall's Resolution

Randall shared that he allowed himself expensive ice cream with sprinkles—lots of sprinkles. When he was a child, these treats were randomly taken away or forbidden when his mother was in a bad mood.

Randall had always wanted a pet, so he got a cat. This was huge, because pets were not allowed in his childhood house, not even fish. He was a kind and loving cat dad, which helped him continue to be kind and loving with himself. Randall stopped calling his anxiety nasty names and started to listen to what it really needed, which was love and comfort. He continued to add skills to lessen his anxiety.

The most useful skill for Randall was learning to dialogue with his anxiety and allowing his anxiety to dialogue back to him. He learned a lot about himself that he was previously unaware of. Randall continued to use the dialogue technique when his anxiety showed up. He found that his anxiety responded to kindness, which surprised him. He admitted his anxiety wasn't always correct, but he was listening. He listened the way his mother was never able to.

He began the process of forgiving the men in his life and started to heal. Randall began disconnecting from his family legacy that had rolled from one generation to the next. The more Randall made connections from his present-day negative criticisms to his past, the less critical he was. As Randall employed more compassionate self-talk, he chose to give up his option of returning to self-hatred.

Summary

Once you start to protect yourself in healthier ways, your negative self-talk will quiet down. As you recover and regain your ability to trust your own voice, you will find you don't need negative self-talk.

Question your negative self-talk. A thought is a thought; some are true, and some are not. You are not obligated to accept thoughts that are not true. You can challenge long-held negative beliefs and identify if they hold up. Learn to release untruths, and replace them with accurate statements that match who you are today. Being your own best friend is important in recovery. You may be used to asking yourself, "I wonder if I will ever feel like I'm enough." The new answer is, "I am enough right now."

If you feed your mind negative self-talk, you will achieve negative results. Shift from, "I can't," to, "I can," and you will find more success. Keep the window to recovery open, because you are just beginning to learn what is possible.

So many times, I have had phone calls from clients telling me they "can't" do the very thing they are doing in that minute. "I am scared" is different from "I can't." The language you use either makes anxiety worse or allows it to disperse.

Give yourself the same kindness and understanding you offer loved ones.

Calm Affirmation

I no longer carry old critical and hurtful comments with me. They do not serve me. I thank them and return them to wherever they came from. I focus on loving and kind self-talk.

Chapter 19
Glitches

> "We have 'glitches' as we move towards recovery. They are part of progress. Embrace them, and they dissipate faster."

Stephanie's Story

Stephanie was experiencing many wins, understanding her struggles, and gaining confidence in recovery by attending our anxiety relief group and practicing her exercises. She reduced her general anxiety and stopped regularly having panic attacks. Stephanie was noticing more calm thoughts in place of endless worry. She practiced calm and focused on the art of sitting through flare-ups without fighting, just allowing anxiety to flow through. Stephanie decided to enjoy even her catastrophic fears as a testament to her vivid imagination. She said yes to her life.

When she hit her first genuine glitch, she felt deflated and wanted to quit. A glitch happens when you are doing well, yet your old pattern reemerges, and your old reactions take over.

She was with friends at a restaurant, sitting outside on the patio, and felt a whoosh of adrenaline. Her anxious mind woke up swiftly, and as the anxiety seeped back in, it was difficult to stay focused on the conversation. She looked for the nearest exit and considered fleeing. Stephanie had enough calm practice to be able to whisper to herself and asked her calm part for assistance. Stephanie put her focus on her hand and began calming her breath. She recalled her three words and grounded herself by putting her hands on her legs. The calm in her was enough to let the flight response disperse.

Back in the anxiety relief group, Stephanie shared the incident and her disappointment about the feelings of panic reoccurred "I quit; I hate this. I was doing great, and now it's back. Maybe I'm not supposed to be calm; I'll just live in my anxious box. I'm a failure. Why is it back?" Stephanie had a glitch.

Stephanie's reaction is common among people who have glitches. Accepting glitches is part of recovery. Stephanie had been successful at bringing her anxiety level down. But Stephanie was shaken, and her frustration reflected her fears that she wouldn't continue to recover. We discussed glitches and how they can be a learning experience about areas that need strengthening.

Skills

Glitches are lessons you need to listen to. A glitch in your recovery shows you which calm skills need strengthening. When you are learning to ride a bicycle and fall off, you get back on and keep going. The scraped knee is painful, but it does not mean you should toss the bike off a mountain and quit. Glitches in recovery are like a scraped knee; it is not a reason to give up.

There are several options on how you can view a glitch. One option is to create a false story to explain your glitch. And, of course, your anxious mind will be happy to assist. The anxious mind's story will be untrue and based in an attempt to protect you from disappointment. But a glitch is disappointing, and you must simply acknowledge it and move on. You can also ask, "I wonder what that was about or why I had a glitch at that moment?" This allows you to be curious and learn from your glitch. Another option is simply to ignore it, accepting it as part of recovery. A glitch is never a reason to criticize and demean your progress.

Recovery does not move in a straight line; glitches are part of your path out of anxiety. Glitches are difficult; they can knock you off your path, becoming a roadblock and stalling progress. It is important to look at your glitches to see what really happened and learn from your glitch. You will find one or more of your skills need additional practice.

Exercise One: Glitch Tracker

Use this tracker to record your glitch and the calm skill that needs strengthening.

DATE	GLITCH DESCRIPTION	SKILL TO WORK ON	SKILL RESULT

Exercise Two: Letter Writing

Letter writing gives you an opportunity to work at a deeper level, open a dialogue between you and your anxiety, and understand it more fully. It can have a profound impact on making your partnership with anxiety more productive. Writing a letter to your anxiety and having your anxiety write a letter to you is one of the most powerful exercises to aid in your recovery.

If you do not think you have anything to say, simply put pen to paper and let it flow anyway.

First Letter

This is from you to your anxiety.

1. Start your letter with, "Dear anxiety,"

2. "It's me." Add your name.
3. Tell anxiety anything you would like.
4. Let it know your true thoughts.
5. Talk about the negative and positive impact anxiety has on your life, work, relationships, etc.
6. As you write, do not worry about editing. Just write.

Second Letter

This is from your anxiety to you.

1. Start with "Dear (add your name), It is me, your anxiety."
2. Let anxiety talk to you.
3. Do not overthink this.
4. You have been listening to anxiety for years.
5. What does anxiety know about you?
6. How long has anxiety been around? What age is it?
7. Does your anxiety have feelings about you?
8. Has anxiety been trying to tell you anything?

Third Letter

This last letter is for you and your anxiety to come up with ideas on how to work together.

1. What do you need from each other?
2. What has been missing in how you relate?
3. What things did you not know that are helpful to see?
4. In what ways can you work together, creating a partnership?

Stephanie's Resolution

Stephanie resumed her practice, focusing on her calm lens. She started with being aware of anxious what-if thoughts related to outings. She chose three outings and practiced maintaining her calm lens while attending. It didn't matter whether it was grocery shopping, walking to the park, or visiting with friends. When she noticed her anxious thoughts, she said, "So what?" Practicing calm allowed her to build her calm muscle and regain her belief in herself.

Stephanie brought herself back to her recovery with a realistic appreciation of glitches. She described her glitches as "little bumps in my road; a hiccup." She wrote to her anxious, scared child part with a letter of forgiveness and recommitted to moving forward. Stephanie found that talking openly about her underlying fear of having glitches allowed her to unhook from them and move forward.

Summary

Glitches are disheartening, and they have the potential to undermine even the calmest person. Glitches are simply a bump in your road; they are not a rupture. It is easy to accept that there will be glitches in theory, but not so easy when it happens. A glitch may shake your calm foundation, tricking you into believing you have no skills and have learned nothing. It is only the moment you are in; it is not a prescription of what will come or a form of punishment. Your skills are still there, even if you did not recall the one you needed most at that moment.

As you practice calm, it becomes a naturally integrated part of you. The goal is analogous to putting calm in the bank so it is readily available when you need it. One of the problematic parts of moving past a glitch is listening to negative self-talk and self-defeating statements again. This is a time to be kind and compassionate to yourself. Use calm affirmations and positive thoughts, and give yourself extra care, not less. A glitch is a moment of discomfort. Have a cry, express your frustration, and keep it in perspective. Use it to identify the skill you need to strengthen and practice that skill, continuously building your foundation of recovery.

Calm Affirmation

I am actively recovering. Every experience is a lesson that makes me strong and calm. I don't judge or criticize my recovery. I am kind and compassionate.

Chapter 20
Feelings 101

Dottie's Story

Dottie, a seventy-eight-year-old woman, contacted me after her friend said, "Dottie, you are the magician of anxiety. I've never met anyone so clever in finding ways to avoid anxiety."

"She was kidding, but it made me realize it was true and my magic wasn't working anymore."

Dottie lived in an independent senior facility. She had instituted all types of "safety valves," as she called them, to manage or avoid her anxiety. She was the designated grocery store driver. "It's not that I am scared to drive; I am scared to be alone in case I get anxious. And the funny thing is, none of my passengers drive anymore, so I don't know how they could help drive if

I needed them to. I have never told any of the group about my anxiety; they might not drive with me."

The thought of going anywhere on her own sent Dottie into a mini panic. In the last couple of years, she noticed the fear of going out alone spread. When the monthly schedule of events came out, she checked to see which of her friends were attending before signing up. "I think it started years ago after my husband died. My doctor told me it was grief, and it would go away. That was ten years ago."

She had struggled with anxiety in her life and knew what this was. "Anxiety was always in my life, mostly in the background. We didn't talk about feelings when I was young. I had an older cousin who was sent to a 'mental institution,' as they were called back then, and my brothers told me if I bothered them, I would be sent there too. That scared me enough to keep things to myself." Dottie's anxiety was generally short-lived and never paralyzing. Avoiding being alone was a major contributor to her continuing low level of anxiety.

What pushed Dottie to get help was an occurrence that happened at the grocery store. The store did not have the particular bread she always bought her husband. She found herself paralyzed with anxiety at the prospect of choosing a different loaf of bread. The longer she stared at the bread options, the more anxious she became. She left the bread aisle, waited for her friends, and drove home.

As she drove back home with her friends, she was aware of a buzz of anxiety. "It felt like I was shaking on the inside. My mouth was dry, and I had trouble following the conversation. I told everyone I was tired.

When I got home, I shut the door and realized I forgot to get any groceries. That anxiety shook me up."

Dottie shared that the day of the "bread incident" was also the day before the anniversary of her husband's death. For the past ten years, she'd purchased his favorite bakery bread and had a slice in his honor. During that ritual, she updated him on all the year's activities as if he were there, raised a piece of bread, and told him she missed and loved him.

Dottie and her husband had owned a business together, raised their family, and were married for forty years. In her mind, it was not rational that she would get anxious over a loaf of bread. Dottie was grappling with an increase of anxiety and sadness and was concerned that maybe she was "losing it." Most days, she couldn't tell if she was anxious or sad or if she was sad because she was anxious. When we met, it was clear that Dottie was experiencing a resurgence of both anxiety and grief.

Dottie's adult son and family were planning a move and asked her to join them. She wanted to be with them, but leaving the area she had lived her entire married life brought up "so much grief for me." She knew she needed to decide. "Every time I try to decide and weigh the pros and cons of the move, I get stuck. My husband, John, would have been the first to tell me to go with them."

Her anxiety was intertwined with her grief, and she needed to process the grief before she could make a decision. She was used to making major life decisions with her husband. "I know it doesn't make sense, but I have this feeling that if I move across the country, my John wouldn't know where I am and think that I abandoned him."

Skill

If we are afraid of our grief or other feelings, we are sending a fear message to our anxiety. Anxiety will rise up to protect us from being overwhelmed by other emotions. We do not need more anxiety; we need to process and experience the feelings anxiety is hiding. Your calm skills support you to do this in a healthy way.

Identify your true feelings. Anxiety is often a stand-in feeling for the real feeling that needs to be expressed. When we suppress emotions, it creates a sense of being off-balance, and that awakens anxiety. When you are unable to be with your true emotions, those suppressed emotions often show up as anxiety. If anxiety is your teacher, it is telling us you are off-balance, hiding your true feelings.

Many people report being frightened of their anger. Anger is not a dangerous emotion; however, putting your hand through a wall is a dangerous behavior. Talking about or expressing your anger in a safe place releases it and weakens its hold on you.

The more you learn about emotions, the better you will express them in a healthy way. This allows you to calm down and face what is driving your anxiety, allowing it to disperse.

Everyone grows up hearing messages about feelings. Many of these messages are incorrect, such as, "Feelings are not important," "Do not express your feelings," and, "Do not trust your feelings."

Because many families did not know how to express their feelings, emotions took a back seat or were identified as bad or wrong. You adopted these messages and instructions about feelings as your own and continue using them today.

You can choose whether to continue to believe those messages about feelings or change them by honoring and talking about your repressed feelings. Once you start talking about them in a safe place, you are sending a loving message that you care about yourself. You will find your anxieties lessen as they no longer need to mask feelings you cannot express.

As you learn about feelings, you will progress through several layers. You may think you are done only to find another major set of feelings to talk about and release. Continue the process of validating your feelings by talking about them and letting them go. This is your path to true recovery.

Exercise
1. What do you tell yourself about your emotional life?
2. What messages did you grow up with about feelings?
3. Are there certain feelings you struggle with more than others?
4. Are your feelings to be trusted?
5. What emotional knowledge is missing for you?
6. Do you have feelings that frighten you or make you feel off-balance?

Find a safe place to talk about and validate your feelings. This can be in a support group, with a therapist, or with a trusted friend. You will be glad you did.

Dottie's Resolution

Dottie lived with the belief that there is a limit to how much, how intense, and how long grief stays with a person. "Everyone goes on with their life after a death. I did also, but my heart is still hurt, and now I believe that grief doesn't go away. I can laugh and find peace and enjoyment, but grief is always with me. That offers some comfort, because it is a connection to John. I do not need anxiety." Dottie made the choice to let her anxiety go by talking about her grief.

Dottie worked on understanding and making connections about what being alone meant for her. She realized that grief and loneliness are different from anxiety. Avoiding her grief fueled her anxiety. The fear that being alone might kill her drove her avoidant behavior. "I held my grief for a long time, but letting it out and crying has been such a relief. And it didn't kill me."

Dottie set up a practice schedule and began trying small activities on her own. She practiced walking to the café alone. She used her three words, being grounded, and her calm lens. As her calm and confidence increased, she took her first solo drive within her neighborhood. Over the next few weeks, she continued expanding the distance, entering a store alone, then shopping.

She was successful in maintaining her calm and decided it was more fun going with her group. The difference was that she made the decision; it was not anxiety's choice.

While we worked together, she established her calm foundation and explored unresolved grief. She brought bread to our last session to declare she was healed. Once Dottie gave herself permission to acknowledge her grief, she was able to move on.

Dottie decided to move with her son's family. She sent me a thank you note with pictures and her gratitude. "I love being with the grandkids. I am glad I didn't let anxiety confuse my decision. There isn't time for anxiety, and I do not miss it." Dottie became involved in a grief recovery support group and enjoys supporting others.

Summary

We are emotional beings. We have over fifty emotions. It is hard to be aware of all our feelings when anxiety is screaming at us. As your calm improves, there will be room for other emotions to emerge.

Grief and other repressed emotions can show up in your life as anxiety. Any emotion you try to run from will eventually outrun you.

Welcome the return of your feelings, and remember that experiencing emotions is part of healing. If you are overwhelmed by your emotions, get professional help. The more you fight emotions, the stronger anxiety becomes. Emotions need to be understood, expressed, and validated as an important part of you.

Calm Affirmation

My feelings are mine to have. They are safe and helpful, and I listen and don't run from them.

Chapter 21
Time to Say Goodbye

Jennifer's Story

"My anxiety and I have been together a long time. I wouldn't say I like it, but I am used to it. It still shocks me how strong my symptoms are even though I have had them for so long. Anxiety has impacted my life in so many areas. I work in an emergency unit at a hospital. Everyone thinks I'm anxious because I work as an ER nurse, but the truth is I love the work. It keeps me distracted from the real anxiety I carry around."

Jennifer seemed resigned to being anxious. "Nursing is stressful, but I can exert control as a nurse, whereas anxiety makes me feel completely out of control. Nursing has never made me want to run out of a building like my anxiety has. My anxious times are work breaks, lunch, and when I am home. When I'm home and get anxious, I want to get under my blanket and not come out."

Jennifer attended a free talk on anxiety and sent an email. It said, "It seems like a long shot for me to ever recover, but I want to try." Jennifer was fifty-five years old and married with two grown kids. She was thinking of retiring but was afraid her anxiety would take over, making her hide under a blanket forever. Her husband had retired and wanted to travel, which was way out of Jennifer's comfort zone. Jennifer had been able to keep anxiety at a distance while at work, so we started with the skills she already had. The most obvious was her courage and creativity.

Jennifer attended the six-week anxiety recovery group. She created three calm words and began using them the minute she got anxious. She posted the words in her house and car. Because she loved music, she came up with a different version of one of her favorite songs to help her stay calm. She sang, "The *Jennifer* will come out tomorrow, bet your *calm* dollar." It worked to calm her anxiety and gave her the confidence she was missing.

She found the "Anxious Me" and "Calm Me" cycles aided her in understanding how she could prevent anxiety from escalating. Jennifer created calm images for retirement and travel. "I noticed the anxious images became dulled in intensity as the calm images were created." She offered her words to other nurses when they needed a little calm.

Jennifer noticed that her breathing became faster and shallower as her workday was ending, contributing to her being anxious at home. She implemented slow, calm breathing on her drive home. As she became more aware of her breathing, she found it calmed incoming patients in the ER. It kept everyone calmer. "By using my calm lens, my days off have been more enjoyable and my fear of staying under the covers does not materialize." Jennifer got involved in art classes and attended local outings. Jennifer was surprised she enjoyed bird-watching.

Skill

Anxiety will listen to you if you are kind, loving, compassionate, and open. Anxiety doesn't listen to begging, threats, or name-calling. Be curious and aware, and you will open an entirely new perspective about anxiety. You'll start to dialogue with anxiety in a way that makes this "enemy" your friend. Once you and anxiety are friends, you will work together with the aid of calm skills.

Letter writing is a useful tool to say goodbye to your anxiety. Doing so helps you let go of it, lessening any of its remaining power. Do not worry if the exercise unearths buried feelings. Anxiety is full of subtleties woven into the fabric of us, integrated in ways that can make it hard to leave behind. Anxiety served a purpose; it makes sense to acknowledge that purpose as you let go.

Exercise

Let your imagination go with this exercise. Don't overthink it. There is no right or wrong way to do this. It is a way to get in touch with any feelings or thoughts you have when you say goodbye and release your anxiety.

Ideas for the goodbye letters are provided. Add, subtract, or change them, and feel free to make it your own. This is about letting your true voice out as you are released from your anxiety. It is ok to express anger, sadness, grief, gratitude, and anything else you need to express.

Goodbye Letter Ideas

Dear Anxiety...

- It is time for us to part.
- Thank you for all you have tried to do.
- You protected me from...
- I forgive you.
- I didn't understand...
- In the future...
- It's time...
- I want you to know...
- Thank you for...
- Have anxiety write to you:
- I want you to know...
- I wish I knew...
- How can I help...?

This can be an emotional exercise; it may take more than one sitting to complete.

Jennifer's Resolution

The hardest part of Jennifer's recovery was letting go. For better or worse, anxiety had been by her side as long as she could remember. "At times, I argued with my anxiety; at other times, anxiety was my closest ally." But as that shifted, she began to think of her anxiety as her scared-kid part. "I can see my anxiety through a different light now. It feels strange and a lot like grief. I cried the other day at the art studio. I have had a lot of losses in my life, and now it feels like I'm losing an old friend—anxiety."

While writing her goodbye letter, Jennifer wondered if she would be lonely or disoriented without anxiety. "As I started writing, I immediately felt a wave of sadness, so I kept going. My sadness was related to how far I have come and for all that anxiety cost me." Jennifer gave herself time to process each section of the writing exercises. "One of my concerns while writing the letter from anxiety was that it would bring it back. Was I jinxing my progress?" Jennifer realized her worries came through her anxious lens, and when she switched to her calm lens, she was able to let go of the fear.

When Jennifer had an anxious moment, she said, "Thank you; I love you." It was still with her, just more balanced. Jennifer continued to allow anxiety to guide her in a gentle way to remind her to keep up her self-care. Jennifer had finally made peace with her anxiety; the fight was over. She had recovered.

Six months after working with Jennifer, she reached out to share that she took a flight to visit her daughter. She had not been on a plane for years and was a bit apprehensive. She had a flash of, "Oh no; what if I get anxious?" Jennifer used her skills and decided, "If I need to buy an extra plane seat for you, anxious one, I will, but I am getting on that plane." Once Jennifer realized she didn't have to hide from anxiety, she felt free of it. She became the one making the decision about how she would react. Jennifer was in charge!

Summary

It may seem odd or counterintuitive to talk about actively saying goodbye to your anxiety, panic, or what-if thinking. Our knee-jerk reaction is, "I want to run from it and never look back." Anxiety has been holding you back, but it has also been trying to protect you.

Anxiety is a lot of things; it's frightening, profoundly limiting, intense, and protective. It was never the enemy. It was always a part of you that kept you off-balance. Recovery means you do not have to run from any emotion. It is a powerful release when you intentionally say goodbye to anxiety.

Feelings are loosened in recovery, which is healthy. You may experience sadness or anger as well as happiness and joy. All feelings are valid. When you suppress emotions, they do not disappear; they simply move underground, waiting to be heard, understood, and released. You cannot be fully healthy when diverting or ignoring feelings.

While saying goodbye to anxiety, you may be concerned about firing up your anxiety again. This is fear talking, and if anxiety gets fired up, you will meet it with all your calm skills until it disappears.

You now have a calm foundation. It will serve you well. Anxiety is no longer needed to protect you. You have a new protector: your calm foundation and all the skills you have learned, practiced, and used to get you through the toughest of times. Congratulate yourself—you deserve it!

Calm Affirmation

I can talk to my anxiety without fearing it. It is not a worry anymore. I am grounded. I am present. I choose to say goodbye.

Chapter 22
Life without Anxiety

Martha's Story

When I met Martha, she was forty-two years old and had been anxious and suffering from panic attacks for a few years. She had anxiety as a young child and again in her twenties. "My anxiety would show up, stay a few years, then quietly leave. It never seemed completely gone." Martha remembers her childhood being filled with activities such as dance classes, guitar lessons, soccer, and ice-skating. She loved being busy and away from home. She had three older brothers; the closest in age was five years older.

Her father began having "anxious spells" while her mother was still alive. He would disappear into his room for hours. Martha would spend time cooking or reading with her mother, which kept her distracted from her father's disappearance. Her mother seemed to accept her father's need for quiet separation, and Martha went along with it. Martha never knew her father suffered from anxiety. "I guess they were embarrassed to tell me or thought I was too young. It just left me confused."

Her mother was in her forties when she gave birth to Martha and was suffering from type 1 diabetes. Her mother died when Martha was seven due to health complications. Martha's father changed after her mother died. He grieved and expressed his sadness. But the anxiety he couldn't talk about, instead taking to hiding in his bedroom.

Her father had more trouble getting to work, and it was unclear to Martha why. All she knew was that when Dad was having a spell, everyone was to be quiet and leave him in his room alone.

Martha remembers being ten years old and falling asleep outside his door one evening. She woke up suddenly, convinced he may have died, but she could not bring herself to break the family rule of going into his bedroom and checking. She returned to her bedroom and cried herself to sleep. "What if Father dies and I could have saved him?" When Dad was present, he was caring and active. He was a graphic artist and loved creating games, trying different art forms, and engaging with Martha.

She felt safe when her father was around and wanted to hold on as tight as she could. Martha wondered if anxiety was a way to stay connected with her father. With her mother gone, she often felt alone, and when her dad hid in his room, she felt unmoored and imagined floating away, convinced no one would notice. She learned to be vigilant to the changes in her father's energy and voice. She was able to identify the moment before he left for his room. She could see him in slow motion as he walked away, but she couldn't do anything to fix him. She made up stories for herself and excuses about him to manage her loneliness and feelings of abandonment. Her prevailing thoughts were, "How could he leave me?" and, "Wasn't I enough?"

The silences and the lack of understanding made living at home unbearable, so she stayed busy, the same as her brothers. Martha was grateful her brothers were willing to drive her to activities. Even though the siblings never talked about Dad's condition, they seemed to understand his need to escape.

It was her sister-in-law who finally told Martha how severe her father's anxiety was. They suspected her father became agoraphobic as he got older. Although the siblings knew he had anxiety, it was the first time someone labeled it and said it out loud. Now they could finally talk about it.

Skill

Letting go of anxiety is a process that incorporates changes in numerous areas. With practice, calm skills will replace your anxious reactions. There are a lot of changes happening as anxiety quiets, including physical, mental, and emotional ones. There is no need to be hypervigilant as what-ifs dwindle and become less important. Emotional changes encompass letting go of and saying goodbye to anxiety. It is more than just anxiety that changes in recovery. It is your sense of who you are now that you are no longer living under an anxious shroud.

Assuming that life will be easy and stress-free once anxiety has lifted is false. Stress is a part of life; it helps guide you. You will need to make decisions in your life. You will manage day-to-day activities. This is all a part of life. The difference is that you will be in control, not your anxiety. Carry your calm skills with you and give yourself permission to grow and find this new footing. Give yourself the gift of patience, acceptance, and gratitude.

Find what you have always wanted to do or be. Recover your dreams. Meet new friends. Try out new hobbies. Do what you've always dreamed of doing. Welcome to your new life!

Exercise

Do you have personal scripts, stories, or narratives about yourself as someone with anxiety?

For example:

Old script: "I was always anxious, even as a kid."

New script: "I have calm skills and understanding now."

Old script: "I take after my anxious mother and her mother."

New script: "I took after my mother as a child. Now I write my new calm story."

Old script: "I always get anxious at the doctor's office."

New script: "Today I acknowledge I do not like the doctor, and I am no longer scared."

Exercise

- Practice writing your new script.
- What is it that you have dreamed of doing?
- What is on your bucket list?
- If you don't have a bucket list, now is a good time to make one.
- What will your life look like without anxiety?
- What have you been restricted from that is available to you now?
- How will you feel, act, and be different?

Martha's Resolution

When Martha and I met, she had just turned forty-nine, the same age her mother was when she died. Her birthday triggered a wave of grief and anxiety. She was familiar with her grief; she was able to take time and let it pass. Grief was easier for her to talk about. Anxiety was the family secret. Martha was unable to keep the door shut on her anxiety. "I was at my desk, and I got flooded with body heat and palpations, followed by trembling hands and disassociation. I knew what it was, I just had not expected it."

Martha needed to disconnect from her father's anxiety and see her experience as her own. He had died seven years prior and sadly was never able to escape anxiety. "If I am anxious like my father, in a strange way, it feels like a secret pact or connection between us. I know he would never want me to suffer like he did. I wish we could have talked about it all."

Martha decided to honor her father by learning to live free of anxiety. "After all, I know he was trying to protect us from his anxiety by hiding it. He would be so hurt to know I carried it into my life."

Martha worked with focus exercises, which helped her stay grounded instead of "floating away." Her three words were *breathe*, *ground*, and *safe*. "I am so accustomed to being anxious and vigilant I don't know how to turn it off." Asking her anxiety what it needed became a morning ritual, replacing her automatic anxious mornings. The answer was often, "I need to stay present."

As Martha's anxiety quieted down, the old childhood feeling of being unmoored slipped away. She was letting go of her what-if thinking and replacing it with, "What if...not."

Martha acknowledged anxiety had helped her through her tough childhood years. She believed it gave her a purpose and aided her need to maintain control. Martha worked on identifying a new purpose for her life that did not leave room for anxiety. She had space to create a new script that wasn't entangled in her father's story. Martha shared her anxiety with friends, further breaking the family secret. She could keep her mother's memory close without feeling anxious and scared. Martha learned to comfort the seven-year-old child without letting the seven-year-old be in charge. Martha's calm lens showed that she was a forty-nine-year-old, successful, independent woman who remained grounded.

Martha decided to return to college and finish the social work degree she had previously abandoned because her anxiety prevented her from graduating. As she reveled in her success, she thought of her father often and wished she could have helped him through his battle with anxiety. She committed herself to sharing the gift of finding peace and healing anxiety with others.

Summary

You are writing a new life script with calm as your new normal. This new way of living may have its challenging moments, but you are now living with calm as your new way of life. You have practiced your calm skills and built a foundation of calm.

These calm skills will be with you forever. You do need to continue practicing these calm skills from time to time to keep them available when you need them most.

Glitches do happen; they happen to every human being on earth—know this. When a glitch does happen, learn from it and return to your foundation of calm.

You have made the transition from living life with an anxious lens to a calm lens. Have patience with yourself, give yourself what you need most, and give yourself the love and kindness you deserve. You are your own best friend; you are the only person who will always be with you. Treat yourself as you would treat the most loved person in your life. You have earned it; it is yours!

Calm Affirmation

I have recovered. I practice calm skills and behaviors. I have found my calm.

SECTION III
Frequently Asked Questions
This section answers many questions from clients over the years.

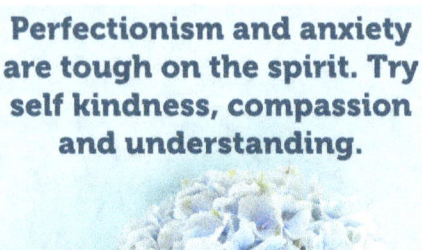

Perfectionism and anxiety are tough on the spirit. Try self kindness, compassion and understanding.

What Causes Anxiety?

To understand what causes anxiety, one must understand what it is. Anxiety is not being able to calm down when you get scared. Being scared is how one naturally responds to danger. People from a thousand different backgrounds have walked through my doors over the years. The one consistent truth is there are many factors that lead to your anxiety.

You may ask, "Is it inherited? Learned? Hardwired? Trauma-related? A reaction to an unstable childhood or bullying?" There are many contributing factors as to how anxiety starts. You come into the world with your own unique personality traits and add them to your family structure and lifestyle. There is not one thing I can equivocally say is the cause of anxiety. I had it; my sister did not.

Whatever the cause, anxiety and panic will not go away if you react to it negatively. The good news is you can learn to change your reactions and say goodbye to anxiety. The one consistent truth is that it is not your fault. You did not deliberately or even consciously create your anxiety. Nobody actively volunteers for anxiety.

I encourage you to find the answer to your anxiety's origins as part of your recovery. Etiology is important, but without learning new ways to relate to anxiety and developing ways to calm your anxiety, the information is not enough.

Anxiety is a self-reinforcing pattern, and it is about not having the skills to calm yourself. The pattern is reinforced when you get anxious or you become scared of being anxious or terrified of another panic or anxious siege—that is what keeps anxiety alive. Break that pattern, and the anxious fire is extinguished.

Anxiety is a perfectly logical reaction to a distorted perception. This can be a difficult concept to wrestle with, given all the chaos anxiety has dumped in your life. The distortions are in the perception of the experience; any real danger or perceived danger is magnified by the addition of anxiety. If you perceive any danger, anxiety will always react accordingly. If you tell yourself, "I am safe," there will be calm—no need for anxiety.

When told there is danger, the anxious mind maintains that belief until evidence to the contrary is presented. You can offer alternatives. Magical thinking tells you that you can prevent catastrophic events from happening simply by worrying. Children use it when they play make believe; they believe what they make up. You can use logical thinking to establish calmer alternatives. Offering factual evidence gently dismantles false and frightening thoughts.

Examples:

Fear talk: "I can't tell you *what* I am scared of, just that I'm scared."

Alternative: "Thank you, and I am safe. I am choosing not to be scared unless there is something specific to be scared of."

Fear talk: "Every time my daughter calls during the day, my stomach jumps to my chest. Is something wrong?"

Alternative: "My daughter has called over a thousand times, and nothing has been wrong. When she calls, I will breathe out and stay grounded."

Fear talk: "I feel uneasy when I get on the highway. What if I have a panic attack?"

Alternative: "I can be uneasy and still drive safely. Feeling uneasy does not mean I'm having a panic attack."

This is a phone call received from a client while she was practicing calm while driving on the expressway:

Client: "I can't possibly drive; any minute, there will be a disaster!"

Me: "Right now, you are driving; let's focus on that. Breathe out. Feel your hands on the wheel."

Client: "It is getting worse; I can hardly feel my legs, and I think I stopped breathing."

Me: "If you truly can't continue, then safely pull off to the side of the road."

Client: "No, I'll keep driving. It would be worse if I pull over. But soon I'll have to pull over so I can breathe."

Me: "It sounds like you are scared, and you are driving safely and breathing."

Client: "How do I know if I stop breathing? It feels like it can stop anytime."

Me: "You are talking, so I know you are breathing. And your fear is making you feel uncomfortable."

Client: "Oh, that's right. Phew. No, I'm a very safe driver when I'm nervous, because I pay close attention. I am ok now."

Once the client had permission to pull over, she felt better. And as she felt calmer, her logical mind allowed her to become unstuck from her anxious mind. Her logical mind knew she was breathing, and it was the discomfort that caused her to breathe shallowly. It is common to say, "I can't do something," in the exact moment you are doing it. Remember, the anxious mind is not a problem-solver; the calm mind is.

When anxiety is yelling at us, we do not hear our calmer self. If you get anxious, it is vital not to make any promises, like:

- "If I get out alive, I will agree to anything."
- "I promise to never shop in this store again."
- "I will never, ever take this road again."

These are links to the next anxious moment. In recovery, you begin to identify and sever connections and anxious links.

Do You Use Fight, Flight, or Freeze?

- If you are a fighter, loosen your grip, drop your shoulders, relax your jaw, and turn your palms up.
- If you run or take flight, try walking slow, slowing your breathing, and feeling your feet on the ground.
- If you freeze, it can be hard to remember what to do. Use your three words, remember you are safe, breathe out, breathe in, breathe out, and focus on your breath, and it will bring you back.

All reactions are temporary. Do not add more fear with what-if thinking.

Have You Tried Mindfulness?

Learning to be mindful is not complicated. You can be mindful anytime while doing anything and for as long or short a time as you choose. The dictionary defines mindfulness as "a mental state achieved by focusing one's awareness on the present moment while calmly acknowledging and accepting one's feelings, thoughts, and bodily sensations. The quality or state of being conscious or aware of something."

It isn't about judgment or whether you like or dislike your state of being. Anxious minds are rarely quiet enough to be mindful. One of the common reactions to anxiety is an immediate scattered feeling. Unless you bring down your anxiety level, you will react: fight, flight, or freeze. Thoughts and fears will flood you as you try and figure out what to do. Those are not mindful states of being. If you use mindfulness instead of fighting, you let go and are present and breathing. No need to make any decisions other than to be present.

Start practicing it. Try it when you are doing dishes, talking to a friend, or petting a dog or cat. You don't have to sit down in a special place; just practice in the moment you are in and the next and the next.

Mindful Practice Tips
- List different places you can practice mindfulness.
- Record progress, what you notice, and what struggles you have.
- Is it difficult to be quiet?
- What do you notice when you are mindful?
- What happens to your body when you are mindful?
- What happens to your anxiety when you are mindful?
- Do you have judgments?
- Are you critical of how you are practicing?

There are many audio resources that teach mindfulness and meditation. Try making your own audio with your voice since you listen to your voice all the time. This is a way to listen to your calm voice. Record your calm voice and listen to it when you are anxious or feeling insecure. It helps integrate the newly found calm part of you more deeply into your senses.

How Do I Get to Sleep?

If you are anxious during the day, it makes sense you will be anxious during sleep. As you awaken, anxiety seizes the opportunity to wake up with you.

Before bed, use your calm lens skill to create the image of a restful night's sleep. Acknowledge what has been happening with sleep, and accept that first.

"I have had trouble sleeping, and tonight I will sleep restfully all night. If I wake up in the middle of the night, I can return to sleep. There is no need to worry about the next day. No decisions need to be made at 2:00 a.m." If you worry that you will forget something, jot it down and return to the image of sleeping. The anxious lens is always available to collect all types of catastrophic possibilities. "What if I don't sleep and I am tired all day, and what if I never sleep again?"

The calm lens provides a different response: "If I don't sleep, I will be tired, and I can still function." The calm lens holds the image of restful sleep; engage that lens.

"I wake up every morning, and the first thing I check is how anxious I am. That sets my day for me." Checking through an anxious lens will guarantee anxiety. It sets you up for looking for anxiety. Switch to the calm lens and predict, "I am searching for calm today. If I am anxious, I have a calm skill to apply. My anxiety is not the boss today." Or "My anxiety feels uncomfortable; it is not dangerous. I am safe. I am repeating my three words and focusing on calm breathing."

Muscle relaxation, music, mindful exercises, and relaxation tapes are all helpful. Create a calming ritual and do the same routine each night. Follow it even if you are not anxious to get in the habit of calming before sleep.

Will Learning Calm Skills Help with Trauma?

One of the questions that comes up repeatedly in sessions is, "I suffer from post-traumatic stress from earlier traumas and have anxiety. Will these skills help?" Absolutely! This book isn't focused on trauma. However, the same skills and calm principles apply. I would like to offer some thoughts and hopefully generate comfort about trauma and how it relates to anxiety recovery.

Trauma is about real danger; it is not a fear of anxiety symptoms or fear of danger. Anxiety can become attached to trauma to protect oneself from unsafe situations. Trauma may end, but anxiety may linger. It is important to separate trauma from anxiety.

When a child has experienced trauma, they learn to protect themselves in many ways. Instead of learning to relax and be calm, the child learns to be hypervigilant, constantly looking over their shoulder. They are in survival mode, and those survival skills carry into adulthood. Anxiety is the siren that tells you there is danger, so it feels safer to keep anxiety alive and at your side.

Many adults talk about not cognitively understanding what was happening when they were young. "I always knew there were bad things going on. When my dad came home drunk, I knew he would be angry. The next day, he acted like nothing happened. My anxiety told me I was right to be scared."

It has been my experience as a professional working with people with trauma that anxiety has to be quieted first. Anxiety is our response to danger, and talking about past dangers can trigger anxiety or panic today. The anxiety becomes so overwhelmingly debilitating that trauma work must be temporarily put aside. "When I have done therapy work on earlier trauma, I get so anxious it is difficult to think. Being told to calm down doesn't help. I feel retraumatized and quit." You need to build the internal calm foundation to support trauma work.

Here are some of the ways the calm skills can help your trauma work:

- Breathing awareness can signal the need for self-care and attention rather than anxiety.
- Creating a safe place offers an alternative when the mind gets stuck in the past.
- Using dialogue and writing exercises keeps people in touch with unexpressed needs.
- Grounding and focus exercises provide a way to stay grounded in the present time.
- Trauma work may need to be sidelined while you learn how to manage anxiety.

Being able to calm the fears while releasing trauma puts survivors in charge. Anxiety's way of protecting is limited to fight, flight, freeze, or avoid, and these techniques are the resolution of trauma. If the focus is on avoiding or managing anxiety, that will be the focus. Work on managing your anxiety symptoms first, then tackle your trauma.

Can You Unconditionally Accept Anxiety?

Can you unconditionally accept anxiety right now, no matter what, without any conditions?

This is an important step to work toward. I did not say, "Do you like your anxiety?" The question is, "Can you unconditionally accept it?" If not, you will waste time fighting with it, trying to control it, hide it, and smash it. You will make mistakes, and there will be glitches, and the more smoothly you ride through them, the sooner you will recover. You need all your energy to become the calm and internally peaceful person you want to be. Using your calm skills and calm foundation reduces the magnitude of your anxiety and enables you to unconditionally accept yourself and your anxiety. Acceptance is vital.

Does Anxiety Distort Perceptions?

If you have a physical sensation like a dry throat and you interpret it as a sign of danger, you will become scared when you have a dry throat. If you look at the same dry throat as a temporary reaction to being thirsty, you could drink a glass of water and be done with the thought.

If you take a deep breath and allow thoughts to pass, they don't become scary thoughts. Thoughts come and go with or without our assistance or interruptions. Perception is crucial to whether you become anxious or stay calm. If you interpret sensations as danger, you will react with fear. If you know you are safe, you can remain calm.

Do You Struggle with Control, Perfectionism, Guilt, and Shame?

These four traits keep people stuck in anxiety longer than necessary.

Control is the opposite of what recovery requires. The more you try to control, the more anxiety you will have. When anxiety strikes, the worst thing to do is clamp down and attempt to prevent more anxiety.

This only builds anxiety. Trying to control your anxiety only increases the amount of time it takes to quiet your anxiety.

Trying to control thoughts is as effective as herding cats. If I say, "Do not think of a swan," it probably took three seconds before a gorgeous swan floated into your mind. Is there a swan anywhere in the vicinity? Do you have a pet swan or pass by swans every day? Is there any reason to conjure up a swan image other than because it was suggested? It wasn't a life-and-death command, just a request not to think of a swan. Our mind has an infinite number of files full of images. We are not consciously aware of all the images and thoughts; they are there if we need them. It seems truly futile to believe we have control over when they pop up. We can learn to focus on a task and ignore an intrusive image. We can learn to minimize the damage of interruptive thoughts. Eventually, they become less of a flashing object as we focus more on calm responses.

It is a false belief to think, "If I think it, think it, think it and hold my fists as tight as possible, I will have control." Trying to avoid anxiety by being tight and restricted brings it on full steam. Recovery comes from unclenching your fists, breathing deeply, and dropping your shoulders, signaling to your body that you are welcoming calm. It is about breathing out, not in. The fight for control does not allow for human error, yet recovery is full of human error. Letting go of control signals that you are safe, thus reducing anxiety.

In certain fields, striving for perfection is necessary, but not in anxiety recovery. We are all wonderful, amazing, and hugely imperfect beings. If you hang on to the need for perfection, happiness will remain elusive; the two cannot exist in the same space. When you reach a healthy state of calm, that old search for perfection will tell you it is not enough, creating doubts about your recovery and again signaling a false belief. Calm is enough.

Guilt and shame both produce anxiety. Guilt means you feel you did something wrong. It takes all sorts of forms—lying, stealing, withholding, cheating. It is generally an uncomfortable feeling attached to a behavior, and if you change the behavior, you can reduce guilt.

Shame is the belief that there is something inherently wrong or bad about you at your core—that you are a bad person.

Shame comes from many sources but leaves us feeling as if we are never enough, or that we are damaged and hurt. Anxiety is a distortion of truth that compounds shame. Shame appears as more evidence that you are broken in some way.

There is nothing inherently wrong with or bad about you. Know that. Shame is a set of interlocking beliefs held in place by underlying emotions. These beliefs can be changed by working through the underlying emotions. Work on separating shame from anxiety. It isn't your anxiety that feels shame; it is you. Having calm skills with a calm foundation quiets the anxiety so the shame can be worked on and released. As anxiety lessens, you have the opportunity to heal your shame and your life.

Can You Shift What-If Thinking to What-If-Not Thinking?

Almost everyone, anxious or not, listens to what-ifs from time to time. "What if this does not work? What if I get scared and panic? What if nobody likes me?" Some people are able to listen and ignore these, yet others are not able to. *What* and *if* are two of the most powerful negative words with endless anxious possibilities. What-if thinking is like a one-hundred-year-old oak tree with thousands of branches. One branch leads to the next, which leads to the next, and so on. The only way to quiet the what-ifs is not to engage with the first branch. See the tree, but do not climb the tree.

When you are invited to a party, the anxious what-ifs will say, "What if I go to the party and no one talks to me, and I have nowhere to sit, and I get embarrassed? And if they do approach, I won't know what to say, because I will be anxious and need to get out, but I will be trapped, and then I will have a panic attack!"

In my years of listening to what-ifs, it became clear that adding the word *not* to the end of "what if," would shift the entire meaning. Using the what-if-not lens offers this slant: "When I get to the party feeling confident and calm, everyone will want to talk to me, and they will all ask me to sit with them, and I will be present, funny, and the life of the party. It will be a great time, and anxiety will be fast asleep at home."

What-ifs are created in our anxious mind as an attempt to control what we cannot. We can use our calm mind to create different scenarios. If you do not try to do things differently, you always get the same old results. You already know that your what-ifs are based in fear, and fear is a liar. This is another calm skill to practice, and it can be fun to imagine incredible outcomes based in joy and happiness.

Think about how many thousands of what-ifs you worried about that did not come true.

How many things have happened in your life that you did not what-if about? When these things happened, you dealt with them. Did any of your what-ifs change the outcome? No!

Practice putting your what-ifs through the what-if-not lens and see how different it feels. "What if this works out and all goes well? What if this is the best job ever, and I am highly successful?" Using "what if not" has the power to change the outcome.

As you get better at making this change, remember this: worry comes and goes. Learn to let it go, and do not follow the worry down the road, off a cliff, and into the river. If you do follow it into the river, please get out of the water, dry yourself off, and wave to worry as it floats down the river by itself.

Am I in Real Danger?

My favorite analogy is about meerkats. They are small mammals that live in groups. They easily get preyed on, so when the group is sleeping or eating, there is always a meerkat lookout standing watch to protect the group. If there is danger, they let the group know. They are constantly on alert as they could be in danger at any time with predators around. Meerkats have real danger in their life. That is the persona you take on when you are scared by your anxiety. You start looking around and being tense, becoming hypervigilant, which makes you susceptible to creative what-ifs and anticipatory anxiety. However, unlike the meerkats, you are not in real danger. Know that, and take comfort in that.

Why Is Car Anxiety So Common?

Many of you have anxiety in the car, whether it is about distance, freeways, or bridges. When you first learn to drive, you must think about each step one at a time—seatbelt on, check mirrors, signal, and slowly move the car forward. Once you know how to drive, you let go and drive, trusting memory and instinct for safety while naturally reacting to the flow of traffic.

When anxiety gets in the way, it is hard to let go of anything or trust yourself. The more you think about driving, the more anxiety you feel. Driving then becomes unnatural and scary. The next anxious step is avoidance or creating comfort zones ("I can only drive to the end of the block. I can only drive my children to school, nowhere else"). Freedom to drive starts being restricted by rules—no driving over three miles, avoid left turn lanes, drive early in the day, cross no bridges.

Following these comfort-zone rules promotes anxiety. The anxious part of you knows you are scared and will remind you every time you get behind the wheel.

All is not lost. The more you practice with calm skills and follow a practice schedule focused on driving, the more you will begin taking back the ability to drive freely, step by step.

Does Luck Have a Role in Recovery?

A client once told me, "I am almost anxiety-free; I could not have done it without you and that little Valium I have carried in my purse for the last twenty years. I even move it from purse to purse so it is always with me." I was surprised, because this individual had mastered all the calm skills, reclaimed her life, and had always been medication-free. "What do you think the Valium is doing for you?"

She described it as her lucky charm. She had worked hard at her recovery. It was possible the Valium wasn't potent after twenty years. The suggestion to get rid of the pill immediately produced an anxious flash. Once she saw it for the back door it was, she knew she really didn't need it and tossed it. This was an important step in her recovery.

The problem with believing in luck or lucky charms is they are based on an external source of false calm. The mind makes connections to manage feelings, but it also gives away the confidence gained by learning to be calm. Even though she never took the pill, her fear-based belief was that it was helping her. And we know fear lies. The twenty-year-old pill did not keep her calm. She didn't need it. She could rely on herself if she got anxious, not the pill.

Luck has nothing to do with recovery; it's about practice and knowledge. Practice your calm skills and build your calm foundation. They are your path to recovery.

SECTION IV:
Welcome to Your Calm Life

Anxiety recovery is about finding and keeping your calm self. It's about building a foundation of calm to replace your anxious foundation. It is about getting your life back. You deserve to be happy. My intention is that you create and define what you need as you work through the process from anxiety to recovery. It may be enough to simply be free of anxious symptoms and live your life through a lens of calm. It may be that you want to reclaim parts of your life that have been diminished by your struggle with anxiety.

Do not be surprised if you experience previously lost emotions during this process. It is natural to feel a sense of sadness related to the things you missed because of anxiety. You may be angry that you ended up with this card in life. Many of the people who participate in the anxiety recovery groups overcome their anxiety and decide to find a therapist or coach to continue their personal growth journey.

Others need to do body work to release the physical strain of being anxious for years. Allow yourself time to understand and process what was lost as you reconnect with your life. In this new phase, accept all your feelings without judgment and criticism.

Which of these areas of your life might need to be addressed to promote balance and well-being?

- Relationships?
- Physical or emotional health?
- Work-life balance?
- What is right in life?
- What is missing?
- What support do you need?

Being an observer of anxiety lets you step back from being an active participant. Being curious means not being scared of anxiety. It means being open and willing to see what it's really about rather than what fear tells you it's about. As you become calm, those points of view will be the natural outcome. Someone with a curious viewpoint would ask, "Oh, I wonder what this flash of anxiety is telling me?" instead of saying, "Uh-oh, something bad is going to happen."

What you say to yourself when you are anxious has a significant impact on how you live with anxiety. If you fight with anxiety, swearing at it and criticizing yourself, you will become more anxious, not less. If you continue to be highly reactive to your world, you will continue to feel unsafe and anxious. The more you are at war with anxiety, the bigger the war. You will always lose the fight with anxiety until you fundamentally view it from a different lens.

When you ignite the anxious part, you are rewarded with more anxiety. Observing rather than reacting will help shed light on the cycle of anxiety. You might not be able to turn the anxious volume to zero immediately. Keep moving from fear to awareness, anxiety to calm.

Remember:

- You did not cause your anxiety.
- It is not about external triggers.
- It is an internal process.
- Self-esteem is the esteem you give yourself.
- Treat yourself as you would a best friend.
- There is no shame in having anxiety.
- Anxiety is a learned response.
- You can learn a new response.
- There is no magic wand, and you don't need magic.
- Be curious.
- Be open.

Walking Out of Anxiety

It took me a long time to understand how my behavior contributed to accidentally walking into anxiety, which was clearly not my intention. It became apparent one day as the store door was opened and anxiety appeared. Where did it come from? It came from the part of my anxious mind that was always on alert, trying to avoid perceived danger. In a moment of clarity, my calm mind provided the suggestion to stop scaring myself. For some reason, anxiety listened, and anxiety was appeased. "If you walk into anxiety, you can walk out."

Calm skills give you the tools to walk back out of anxiety and to stop scaring yourself. Anxiety follows the anxious trenches you have been walking through. When you respond with anxiety, you get more anxiety. When you use calm responses, you get calmer. Sometimes, it is that simple!

It Is Safe to Tell the Truth

No one likes the symptoms of anxiety and panic. It feels scary, uncomfortable, and icky, yet the symptoms are not dangerous. That is the truth, and you can tell that truth.

Fear has been lying. It is also trying to protect you, but it has a distorted view of the truth, and you can use logic and calm to know fear is lying. It is important that you don't lie to yourself about how the symptoms feel.

"Don't make a big deal about being a little nervous. Everyone feels nervous. It's not real." If you have heard that from others, ignore it; it is real. Acknowledge your truth. Symptoms do not give you a warm, cozy feeling. This is not about feeling a little nervous.

Acknowledge that you are not in danger and you can get through it. You are still here; you have had many anxious and panicked moments, and you are still here. This is not your first panic party. Anxious thoughts can be countered with calm thoughts. Instead of letting anxiety run rampant, switch to calm alternatives:

- "I have been here many times. Today, I will breathe through it and let go."
- "I know my anxiety thinks I'm in danger, and I know I am safe. I'll let her know."

When you acknowledge what you are experiencing, you have a better chance of shifting away from anxiety. The goal is to move toward calm and away from anxiety. In any anxious situation, you can focus energy toward calm. You are learning what calm looks like, how it feels, and which calm skills to employ to reach calm. You are now able to move from anxiety to calm, from shallow breathing to slow breathing, from feeling lightheaded to feeling grounded.

The more focus, attention, and worry you put toward anxiety, the more anxiety you have. The same is true of calm. Focus on calm to have more calm.

Give Yourself Time to Recover

Anxiety is a pattern that can develop over time or can happen suddenly. It is not always screaming or loud. Anxiety happens in small, subtle ways. It develops in the way you talk to yourself or in what you avoid or hide from. It happens when you create restrictive comfort zones, negotiate with it, and emotionally beat yourself up for it. It happens as the body becomes reactive and hyperalert. If anxiety has become your go-to response, it will take patience to break the pattern.

Recovery is about breaking old habits and building new ones. Let it breathe with you; let yourself flow. Control is not your friend.

In the past thirty years of working with others, I have learned a great deal about the nature of anxiety, panic, and related issues. There are many paths out of anxiety. Find yours.

As anxiety chatter becomes quieter, it is easier to talk with your calm part when you feel uneasy. Your mind is used to listening to the fears the anxious mind has been sharing. Now, there is room for calm talk. Ask your calm part to let you know how it can help.

My Wish for You

You now know fear is a liar. It misinterprets information and tries to protect us in primitive ways. Thank it, and do not let fear steal any more of the joy in your life. What-if thinking projects future worry, if-only thinking holds on to past regrets, and the only place to be calm is in the present.

Find your true self and your passion; let them soar. This is my hope for you. This is your time.

Please, please don't give up. I lived with anxiety and panic, and I have lived without. Living without anxiety is my wish for you. You have more important things to do in life than being anxious. It is time for you to shine. No more shrinking with the pressure of anxiety. Make this the time you extinguish your anxious fire once and for all.

================THE END =================

About the Author

Barbara Spaulding, LCSW, has been a dedicated counselor and life coach since 1985. She earned her Master's in Social Work from Loyola University and furthered her education at the Family Institute of Chicago. Barbara has extensive experience in various clinical and managerial sectors of social work. Since the 90s, she has been leading a private practice group of incredible therapists, offering counseling for individuals and families. Barbara teaches her Anxiety Relief skills in groups and on meetup.com. Barbara's personal life is filled with love for her family, friends, pets, various crafts, books, exploring and walking.

barbspaulding@hotmail.com
www.anxietyandpanic.net
https://www.facebook.com/groups/230253820645086
Instagram
https://www.instagram.com/barbspauldinglcsw
https://www.tiktok.com/@barbaraspauldinglcsw

www.ingramcontent.com/pod-product-compliance
Lightning Source LLC
LaVergne TN
LVHW021951060526
838201LV00049B/1670